Learning
═to═
Die

Learning
═ to ═
Die

Samuel Gerber

Translated by Peter J. Dyck

HERALD PRESS
Scottdale, Pennsylvania
Kitchener, Ontario
1984

Library of Congress Cataloging in Publication Data

Gerber, Samuel, 1920-
    Learning to die.

    Translation of: Sterben will gelernt sein.
    Bibliography: p.
    1. Death—Religious aspects—Christianity—Meditations.
I. Title.
BT825.G3913   1984   248.4   84-10809
ISBN 0-8361-3369-2 (pbk.)

LEARNING TO DIE
Copyright © 1984 by Herald Press, Scottdale, Pa. 15683
    Published simultaneously in Canada by Herald Press,
    Kitchener, Ont. N2G 4M5. All rights reserved.
Translated from the German book, *Sterben will gelernt sein,*
copyright by Brunnen-Verlag Basel, Switzerland.
Library of Congress Catalog Card Number: 84-10809
International Standard Book Number: 0-8361-3369-2
Printed in the United States of America
Design by Alice B. Shetler/Cover photo by Camerique

90 89 88 87 86 85 84 10 9 8 7 6 5 4 3 2 1

Contents

Preface to the English Edition – 7
Author's Preface – 9

1. Dying Can't Be Avoided — 13
2. The Bottom Line — 17
3. Learning to Die — 22
4. The Essential Foundation — 27
5. The Liberating Fact — 32
6. Too Good to Be True? — 37
7. As We Live, So We Die — 42
8. Strangers and Pilgrims — 51
9. Practical Matters — 56
10. Learning to Let Go — 61
11. The Last Hours — 66
12. Gratitude Dispels Bitterness — 70
13. How to Handle a Dying Person — 72
14. The Process of Dying — 77
15. Christian Assistance to the Dying — 82
16. The Sacredness of Life — 85
17. The Right to Die — 89
18. Expecting to Die — 94
19. Orientation for Heaven — 99

Other Resources on Death — 104

Preface to the English Edition

My brother-in-law C. F. Klassen and I were driving through a dark night in Europe in 1945. Death was all around us. The darkness seemed greater than that caused by the absence of sunlight. The global conflict of World War II had destroyed everything: family, cities, dreams, and hopes for a brighter future. In the rubble of the ruins we had been looking for refugees.

Presently Klassen, the MCC (Mennonite Central Committee) director for Europe, turned to me and asked, "How are these people ever going to put their lives together again?"

After many miles of pondering this question he answered it himself. "The people have to come under the Word," he said, a rather literal translation of "Die Menschen müssen unters Wort kommen!"

Samuel Gerber was the man whom God and the international Mennonite community chose to bring that about.

By profession a teacher and minister, Samuel Gerber, father of five children, has been principal for more than 25 years of the European Mennonite Bible School at Bienenberg near Liestal, Switzerland. The objective of the school and of Samuel Gerber has been to bring young, and not so young, Mennonites and other Christians "under the Word." The motto of the school is "With joy you will draw water from the wells of salvation" (Isaiah 12:3).

In this book, *Learning to Die,* Samuel Gerber looks at death and the preparation for dying in the light of Scripture. In doing so he follows the example of his Swiss forebears who always asked when questioned about faith and life, "What does the Bible say?" The book contains many positive suggestions on the lifelong process of learning to die.

I enjoyed translating the book. I have been blessed by it. With all my heart I join Samuel Gerber and the ancient psalmist who prayed: "So teach us to number our days that we may get a heart of wisdom" *(Psalm 90:12).*

Peter J. Dyck
Labor Day, 1983

Author's Preface

"Dying is not child's play." How often I heard my father say that when he was called to the bedside of a dying person. Learning to die is something we all should start practicing early in life.

Persons who have not learned to die will die anyway, just like everyone else, but their last hours will be extremely difficult for them and their loved ones. We do not want to avoid the fact of death. We want to think about dying before it is too late. May God help us.

Some time ago I spoke in a series of meetings on the theme "So teach us to number our days." Many people said afterward that these messages on dying held a special attraction for them, and that they were thankful for the faith-building experience. Later I adapted that series for my radio ministry.

I hope and pray that these thoughts now in printed form will encourage many people to think more deeply and honestly about dying. May the words of Paul be realized in each one of us when he said, "It is my eager expectation and hope that I shall not be at all ashamed, but that with full courage now as always Christ will be honored in my body, whether by life or by death" (Philippians 1:20).

Samuel Gerber
Switzerland

Learning
≡to≡
Die

CHAPTER ONE

DYING CAN'T BE AVOIDED

M oses, one of the greatest men of ancient times, wrote a beautiful song about the frailty and futility of human life. He concluded it with the words, "So teach us to number our days that we may get a heart of wisdom" (Psalm 90:12). Isn't it strange that a man so great, a real man of God "whom the Lord knew face to face" (Deuteronomy 34:10), had the feeling that there was still one more lesson that he needed to learn, a dark chapter that he did not yet understand?

Yes, Moses knew what he was talking about. During his long life he saw tens of thousands of people die. People are like wilted grass. A life is actually little more than a fleeting breath.

People who have often looked death in the face, who have seen many people die, sometimes appear somewhat strange. Unfortunately, nowadays death is removed from us. We don't have much opportunity to witness it. I frequently meet older people who say, "I have never seen a person die." Still less do we have the opportunity all alone to accompany a dying person in the last hour of life.

My father sat beside many deathbeds. He watched ten

of his own children and his first wife die. As pastor he was with many members of his congregation when they died. He tried to walk this last and lonely mile with each one of them as far as he could. One could sense that my father was familiar with death. There was a strange clarity about his life. It had a breath from another world. Because he knew how difficult and how wonderful dying could be, he faced life with deep reverence and with firm determination. He knew that he himself could be called home at any time. He was, in fact, learning to die.

We should all do that. We need help for our own dying, and we should be able to give loving assistance to others when their time for leaving this world comes. It is shocking to see what stupid things people will do at the approach of death. They lie to each other. They become concerned about totally worthless things and forget the most important. Fear and a bad conscience make them rise up and rebel against death. And when death does come, the survivors are plunged into dull mourning and hopelessness, or they arrange for a magnificent funeral as if tears, black clothes, and eulogies about the deceased person can compensate and make right what was left undone in life. Over many graves one should cry out, "Too late!" Too late for the one that died, and too late for those who stay behind.

Dying needs to be learned. "So teach us" is the prayer of the psalmist. Teach us that we have to die. Teach us how to die. Teach us to die in peace. These are difficult lessons, because dying is not child's play.

It is absolutely necessary to think about dying and to talk about dying. In recent years many articles and books about dying have appeared—books about life after death, and books about spiritual counseling of the dying. The theme of assistance in death is almost fashionable. Any number of books have been published about assisting with and relating to the dying, and many authors are becoming more insistent that it is necessary to talk with the dying themselves about death. One senses that it is not so much the dying who don't want to talk about death. Often it is the healthy ones who are too cowardly to open the subject. Because of this new insight many hospitals at last have switched to telling the patient in a loving manner the full truth, instead of playing games or lying to them in their last hour.

Other voices, however, are still quite strong—voices that say, "Talking about death doesn't help. We should talk about life. We should turn our back on death and have nothing to do with it. One has to fight for life. The dying should not think about death. We should nourish thoughts about life in them, otherwise they die too soon." That is why many people continue to make a detour around this delicate subject.

Is it right to talk about dying? Why not follow the Bible in this matter too? The Bible mentions death and dying hundreds of times. It speaks soberly and openly about the subject. Death is not glossed over or treated lightly in Scripture. It is described as an enemy. But the Bible also shows us how we can be liberated from the fear of death. If we stick to the Bible, we *have* to talk about dying.

There is still another reason for considering the topic of dying. Nobody can say, "That's none of my business!" Now if I were to talk about getting married, many people could turn me off, either because they're already married or because they have no intention of ever getting married. But we all have to die. The Bible says everyone must die once (Hebrews 9:27). Death is like a gate we all have to pass through. There's no use resisting or struggling against it. Everyone, including the last person, has to go—the king and the slave, the millionaire and the beggar, the senile old man and the sports-loving, healthy youth. The one is glad for it and the other is horrified; yet both must go. I know of a rich man who never visits sick people and studiously avoids funerals. In fact, he avoids all thought and talk about dying. But it's no use. Sooner or later it will be his turn.

Furthermore, in the matter of dying it is not possible to do what we so often do in various other situations of life— that is, try it once and if it doesn't work the first time, try it again. No way. We die only once! Dying is the bottom line. It is good-bye for good. We all know this, but we don't want to think about it.

My dear friend, when you die the sun will continue to rise. People will continue to love and hate, laugh and cry. The fruit trees will blossom. The cars will zoom along. Wars will rage on. But you won't be there. For a little while they will miss you, but the world won't stop. Even when a great and mighty world leader dies, how soon is he forgotten and replaced?

When we die our life has been fulfilled. What has been has been. No word, no deed, can be erased. What we neglected to say or do can never be made up. No words of love can reach the dead mother. She doesn't hear them anymore.

Yes, dying is a serious and sacred business. We do well to remember that.

CHAPTER TWO

THE BOTTOM LINE

Our turn to die will come too. In fact, the day of our own death is as inevitable as the setting of the sun. And when our last hour comes, our life will have reached its final and unalterable form.

Naturally the world keeps right on turning without any sympathy or feeling. When a person dies it is possible that this is a major catastrophe for the members of the family, but just a few houses down the street nobody pays any attention to it. We are mowed down, yet history goes right on. But the one history, the history of the one who died, has reached its final conclusion. After that nobody can change anything.

Why do I talk about such self-evident things? Because it seems essential to me that we understand the situation correctly. We must stop repressing unpleasant facts. We must comprehend what a serious matter it is, that with our last breath our life has received its final and unchangeable form.

Compare your life with a thick book. Your dying will be its last page. And that's the final script. You cannot remove a page. The blotched and unsightly pages, the botched and embarrassing pages—they all stay. Even if the words "settled" or "finished" are written across the page, it's still there. Nor will you add another page—no, not even another sentence or word.

Perhaps there's a chapter missing that should have been included. You should have said or done this or that yet. To leave that out will be catastrophic. But as soon as you die you can add nothing, absolutely nothing to it. Between birth and death, there it is, the finished and final book of your life.

Isn't this bottom line of your life, your dying, serious enough that we should talk about it? Shouldn't we muster the courage and honesty at least to try? And of course, it would be best to do it with the help of the Bible.

Scripture tells us all persons must die. There's only one exception. When the Lord returns, then those believers who are alive at that time will be "changed, in a moment, in the twinkling of an eye." Instead of being "unclothed" they will be "further clothed" (2 Corinthians 5:4). They will be the only ones who will be spared death; but for them too the moment will come when their last page in the book of life will have been written and nothing, absolutely nothing, can be changed (1 Thessalonians 4:15-18).

However, on the basis of Scripture, we need to say clearly that dying is not a natural process. To be sure, there are those who fantasize about the eternal cycle of nature. Plants, animals, and people are destined to grow, blossom, perpetuate themselves, then wilt and return again to earth. That is the eternal youth of nature with its perpetual renewing process and nothing that is alive can escape it. And of course, to blossom is more pleasant than to wilt. We'll just have to accept that.

To be sure, there is a kernel of truth in this. The world is that way. But the Bible says God has a different intention and purpose with mankind. He did not plan to have us bloom and blossom for a few years and then disappear forever. Death comes into the world as something horrible and dreadful. According to Romans 6:23, "The wages of sin is death." Death is not a natural culmination. Death is an enemy, a destroyer. Death is the payment of a debt, a deserved fate.

Against this dark and dismal background the good news of the gospel shines all the brighter. It will not stay that way. God has a purpose and goal. The time will come when there will be no more death. God will abolish death. The day will come when the last person will have gone down that difficult path of death. Then nobody will die anymore because death will be no more. All creation which is now still subject to death is waiting and "groaning in travail" to "be set free from its bondage to decay," free from the last enemy—death (Romans 8:19-23).

Those who know about this new beginning have already lost their biggest fear of death. Almost mockingly Paul was able to say, "Death, where is your sting?" (1 Corinthians 15:55)

However, until now death still confronts us as a bitter enemy. He is by no means the sweet friend about whom some visionaries romanticize and sing. Soon he will be disposed of for good. Jesus has conquered death. On the third day his grave was empty. Death could not hold him.

However, the reason we need to occupy ourselves with dying is not only because it is such a serious and final matter, but more importantly, because after that comes the big reckoning. "It is appointed for men to die once, and after that comes judgment" (Hebrews 9:27).

If death were the end of it all, the most we could do would be to bemoan the fact that the lovely play is over. But what makes dying so awesome is the fact that after that we have to give an account of our life before God. The Bible speaks very clearly and earnestly about the last judgment.

Yes, God is holy and just. He has appointed a day of judgment on which all the dead will be judged according to their deeds. How meticulously accurate that process is going to be Jesus hinted at once when he said, "I tell you, on the day of judgment men will render account for every careless word they utter" (Matthew 12:36). Should we not read words like these with apprehension and fear? What is going to happen to us preachers and teachers who have spent our lifetime talking?

God will be accurately informed about our life. There will be no need to investigate. Our life will be before him like an open book, including all those dark and shady chapters that were never settled and properly dealt with, all these messy affairs over which the grass has grown a long time. He knows it all.

Why not accept the fact that you are responsible for all of your life? Your life story is going to be reviewed once more in an instant replay by God. You don't need to have been a swindler or scoundrel. You will see who you really are and get a proper perspective on your life when you honestly think about dying. Even good people will be gripped by massive regrets. Suddenly they will realize, "I've been so dumb! I've lived totally wrong! I chased after worthless things and neglected the most important of all. I have been concerned about things that weren't worth it, mere junk which in the light of eternity melts away like snow in the sun."

In a hymn we sing,

> Almighty Maker of my frame!
> Teach me the measure of my days,
> Teach me to know how frail I am,
> And spend the remnant to Thy praise.

Oh, if only we would contemplate more seriously on our value system, on how the many things that we chase after in life appear in the light of eternity. How often would we then pass over things lightly that worry us today? How we would zealously concentrate on questions which we have neglected until now, questions which will rise up with devastating destructiveness against us on the day of judgment?

The remorse of a dying person should not grip us only in our final hour. With all our heart we need to pray, "So teach us to number our days that we may get a heart of wisdom."

CHAPTER THREE

LEARNING TO DIE

There's *Lots of Time Yet to Die* is the title of a book which reports about young soldiers who are mowed down by bullets one after another at the front. Every day some do not return from their engagement. Everyone has to reckon with the fact that he too will soon be among the dead. But they are so young. Life is so beautiful, and dying so horrible. How can they think about dying so early in life? A hundred times they have seen their comrades die. They know what dying is like—and yet they do not know. Somehow each one of them tries to convince himself that he will escape death—until the burning heat of the bullet and the agonizing pain in his body suddenly makes him realize: Now it's my turn!

We should all prepare to die because none of us knows who is going to be next. Suddenly we realize that we are being spoken to very personally. The horrible, bony finger of the reaper is pointing directly at us. And we have to go with him through the dark gate. Will we be able to do it?

Have you ever experienced how another person close to you was suddenly confronted with the reality that he would soon have to die? There are shocking reports about people who were told by the doctor or by relatives that they had only a few hours, a few days, or weeks to live.

Years ago a young minister was giving a week of lectures at Basel, Switzerland. While there he was suddenly gripped by a fatal sickness. The doctor determined that he could be expected to live only a few more days. A friend brought the news to the patient. A sudden terror gripped him. Fear was written on his face. After a while he burst out: "So now it's my turn to die! Please leave me alone until I call you." The minister was a deeply spiritual person. He had preached the good news which takes away the fear of dying to many people. But when the news of his own imminent death reached him like a bolt of lightning out of the clear blue sky, his heart rebelled. He himself had to learn how to die.

For a long time it was very quiet in the room. About two hours later the patient knocked on the wall. His friends came in and found him serene and almost happy. The inner struggle was over. Far away from his own family and loved ones, he had said yes to his early death. He still had time to take care of a few details and then he quietly awaited the last hour.

Yes, we really do have to learn how to die, and this is a lesson that is as difficult for the old as for the young.

Frequently when I walk in a funeral procession I quietly think about who might possibly be the next person whom we will carry to his last resting place. Usually I have thought about my old friends and seriously ill acquaintances and tried to figure which one of them might be next. I have never yet guessed right. Can we imagine how startled the bereaved at a funeral would be, how panic would grip them, if a voice were suddenly to announce who the next person will be to lie in the coffin!

Once on my way to a funeral in Frankfurt, I thoughtlessly crossed the street when the light was red. I was in a hurry and didn't even notice the serious mistake I was making. Suddenly I heard the voice of the police boom over the loudspeaker: "I am speaking to the gentleman in the black suit. You seem to be going to your own funeral!" Long afterwards I could still hear those words in my ears. I had been a hair's breadth away from my own death.

To be prepared for dying does not mean, however, that we are constantly expecting to die or that we wish we could die. We can enjoy life and all that it has to offer. Every normal person has the will to live. Especially the patient needs the will to live in order to conquer the destructive forces in his body. It certainly would not be a healthy nor a biblical attitude if young people would rather die than live. Old people may be tired of life and wish to go home. But anyone in the prime of life does not need to be ashamed of the joy of living.

A young teenager once supposedly complained to her pastor, "Something is missing in my life. I have no desire to die."

The pastor asked, "But why do you need that? Do you have cancer or some other deadly disease?"

The young lady replied, "No, that's just it. I enjoy life so much that I can't say with Paul, 'To die is gain.' "

The pastor laughed and said, "What you need today is not a desire to die. God will give you that and the joy to go with it when the time comes. Today he has given you the task and the joy and the courage to live a full life."

Yes, it can be too early to anticipate death joyfully, but it is never too early to prepare for death. "So teach me to number my days, that I may get a heart of wisdom" is a good prayer also for young people.

Let me mention one more reason why we should learn early how to die. The Bible says that the fear of death makes us slaves, and puts us in bondage (Hebrews 2:15). Fear of death is like a chain attached to our feet. Those who fear death are not free. Suppose someone comes to a crossroads. He sees that the one road is right and the other is evil, but he also realizes that if he takes the right road it will cost him his life. Because he is afraid of death he chooses the evil road.

I've heard people more than once excuse themselves when they had been in a dangerous situation and chosen the wrong road say, "If I had chosen the other road I wouldn't be alive today." But if Jesus has freed us from the fear of death then no one can force us to do evil. Why is it that so many people who make a good beginning end in failure? Because they disobey God and their own conscience. Because they do what their colleagues, their boss, or their secular government ask of them, even if it is wrong and evil.

How different were the three friends of Daniel. In a furious rage the king commanded: "If you do not worship my image, you shall immediately be cast into the burning, fiery furnace."

But they answered, "We have no need to answer you in this matter. God can deliver us, and if he does not do it, we are ready to die."

We must never be so attached to life that we run the risk of breaking God's commandments only to save our own skins. In a time when proof of our faith may be asked of us sooner than we think, should we not occupy ourselves much more with thoughts about dying? As Christians we need to be prepared, if necessary, to give our life for the sake of Jesus. A freedom fighter of our time writes, "It is necessary to say good-bye to life before the police knock on the door; otherwise you are gripped by panic and become a traitor."

If Jesus liberates us from the fear of death by giving us the real life, then we are free indeed and no longer bound by chains of slavery. No power in the world can then force us to do evil. To do evil is no longer an option, because we have learned to die. Death is no longer the worst thing that can happen to us, because Jesus our Lord has conquered it.

CHAPTER FOUR

THE ESSENTIAL FOUNDATION

It is not pleasant to talk about dying, but it is necessary. In spite of medication to ease our last hours, dying has become more difficult nowadays. There is more fear of death and more loneliness in dying than ever.

In most hospitals people die alone. The bed is pushed into a dimly lit room and from time to time an attendant looks in to see whether the patient is still breathing. I know nurses who have never had an opportunity to be with a dying person. Some hospitals would just as soon keep the relatives away from the dying person. Visitors simply make more work. If the last struggle with death happens to be a drawn-out affair, most patients die absolutely alone.

Fortunately, however, there are people today who make every effort to ease the hour of death, both physically and spiritually, for the patient. To be able to give real and practical help to a dying person, it is essential to have thought through for oneself this dark and painful topic. One has to look into the dark abyss oneself—if possible even walk down into the valley of death personally as far as possible.

Those who dare descend into the valley need a strong rope and a sure rock to which it can be fastened. Otherwise, as one looks into the depths, one may be seized with horror and in the end plunge into the deep oneself.

In any event, it is sound advice for all our counseling and spiritual ministry to make absolutely sure that we are securely tied to the rock. Before our words lead people to the frightening precipice of sin, before we invite them to look down into the depths of destruction, we should make sure that we, as well as they, are securely tied to the rock of our salvation. Otherwise, we may only frighten them without really offering help. In fact, it can actually be dangerous to start dealing with sin without being firmly anchored to the rock.

The same is true when we think about dying. We will only increase the fear of dying or else promote a false security and carelessness if we are not firmly tied to the rock of our salvation.

We tie ourselves to the victory of Jesus Christ. This is to be our inner certainty, even when later we speak about outward things, about practical measures to be taken before and during the hour of dying. Jesus Christ died for us. He suffered death and conquered it. He rose victorious from the grave. This truth is never more important than in the hour of death.

That is why it is important first of all to meditate on the death of Jesus. This is an important exercise for our own spiritual maturing as well as for a fruitful ministry; we must comprehend more deeply the death of Jesus. We need to probe more into the mystery of Golgotha. That will strengthen and purify our faith. It will give wings to our adoration and worship. It will continually give a freshness to our life and service.

We are never finished with the cross of Golgotha. There is no way we can fully understand it. Nevertheless, we should attempt as long as we live to comprehend the suffering of Jesus, not philosophically, but listening to and meditating upon the passion texts. In this discussion we will limit ourselves to those texts and truths that are important for the topic of dying.

1. *Jesus died as a human being.* Jesus is the son of God. He knew that his dying would simply be the passing into glory. His victory over death was sure from the beginning. One could therefore imagine that for Jesus, dying must have been easy, somewhat like a surgery for ourselves when we have been given every assurance that we're going to come through just fine. But Jesus agonized over his death the same as any other person. He was afraid. He suffered pain. He was weak. He didn't die smiling like a semi-God, and there was no trace of mockery as of one superior to the experience. He did announce that soon he would be with the thief in paradise, but he died in excruciating pain. The Bible tells us that he cried out loudly. In former times a cross was held before the eyes of a dying person as if to say, "Look at this cross. Jesus, your Lord, suffered just like you do." The idea was not without merit.

2. *Jesus died innocent.* No person has ever died completely innocent. Many have been falsely accused and even illegally executed, but no one has ever died completely innocent. The only one who never deserved death was Jesus Christ. None of us is fit for the kingdom of God the way we are, but Jesus was.

If all of humanity had to appear before the judge of the world and he would pronounce the verdict of guilty on one after the other and hand us over to the executioner, we would have to accept it. We deserve it. Only Jesus did not. He was without sin. But even for him, the innocent one, God saw fit that he should die. How can we, who are guilty, expect to escape death?

3. *Jesus died in great pain.* There was no attempt to execute Jesus as painlessly as possible. They crucified him. His body was stretched out, his hands and feet painfully pierced. In the hot noonday heat he hung on a rough cross bothered by flies, pierced by thorns. The blood in his eyes blurred his vision. He suffered indescribable pain. All the time he was fully conscious. He cried out, "I am thirsty!" But he accepted the pain. He suffered for us! He took upon himself what we deserved.

4. *Jesus died praying.* In the hour of his death Jesus did not sing hallelujahs. He prayed the psalms of suffering. That is why he can assist us today to endure our own pain in dying. Jesus did not accuse God. He prayed in life, and he prayed in death. Even in his last desperate cry we sense something of this, as if he were saying: "My father, you seem to have left me, but I will yet throw myself into your arms."

Happy are we if at last in the hour of death we learn to pray. However, it is much better to practice praying long before that. Then we know that, should the time come when we can scarcely breathe a word, God will hear us and take us safely through the valley of death.

5. *Jesus died working.* Strangely enough, the word "dying" is a verb, although persons who die are usually not active except in cases of suicide. Normally we are being killed by a disaster, an accident, or by other people. We endure death.

But Jesus worked even though his hands and feet were nailed to the cross. That becomes especially clear when reading chapters 18 and 19 in the Gospel of John. The authorities arrest him. The soldiers tie him up. They led him to the trial and finally to Golgotha where they nailed him to the cross. But all the while he was working. He was annulling the old covenant, giving sin its deathblow. He was fighting with the devil. He was concluding a new covenant with humanity. He tore the veil in two. He locked the gates of hell and opened the door to heaven. Because in his suffering and death he worked for us, we are saved. His death brought us life.

CHAPTER FIVE

THE LIBERATING FACT

Nobody can fully comprehend the mystery of the death of Jesus. Again and again we attempt to understand at least that which the Bible explains. We stop in amazement when we consider how Jesus, though he was fully human, suffered with indescribable patience, always praying, and as the innocent one, bearing our load of guilt. And we believe that his death triggered enormous consequences even in the next world.

The Bible says that: through death Jesus destroyed him who has the power of death, that is, the devil (Hebrews 2:14). It tells us that the reason the Son of God appeared was to destroy the works of the devil (1 John 3:8). A wonderful expression of this is also found in Revelation 12:10: "For the accuser of our brethren has been thrown down, who accuses them day and night before our God."

Until the hour when Jesus died, death had unlimited power over people. And the ruler who had power through death was Satan. He is by no means merely a myth. According to the Bible, the devil is a person, a fallen angel. His character, intentions, and objectives are clearly described. He is the father of lies and a murderer from the beginning (John 8:44). He wants to destroy us and cast us into death. He concentrates on our downfall, and since the original Fall, he has the right and the power to do that. People are his victims, and once he has caught them in his clutches he never lets them go again voluntarily.

God's Word says many times that people will need to appear before the judgment seat of God to be judged. Now imagine a scene in a courtroom. Behind the barrier sits the judge. In front of him stands the accused. Beside him or behind him the lawyer takes his place. On the other side of the podium is the prosecuter, the accuser. He has carefully gathered all the material to be used against the accused. He points out which laws the accused has broken and demands a stiff penalty. When the verdict has been pronounced the court police step forward to lead the condemned person away and carry out the sentence.

A similar scene takes place in the unseen world. The Bible says that the devil appears in the courtroom of God as the prosecuter. He is the archenemy of people. He works systematically to destroy them.

The devil is a terrible accuser. First he deceives people, and then he twists his deceptions into a cord with which to hang them. Most of all he hates Christians, those people who reject his power and rule, and who frustrate him in his evil enterprise. He is raving mad at sincere Christians. He will not admit that they are just. He wants to recapture them for his own purposes and put them under his own whip. He tries every trick possible to present the believers before God as hypocrites and failures.

Unfortunately, we have often made his business easy

for him. We have given him more than enough material with which to accuse us. All he needs to do is scan the pages of our book of life, and there they are, long and terrible lists of accusations against us.

What a frightening thought to see ourselves as the accused standing before the holy and just God with the devil, that liar and enemy, as our prosecutor. That's how it was until Good Friday. The devil accused us day and night before God. He was ready to snatch us at any moment, certain that he would claim us as his victims for hell.

But that is gone once and for all. The place of the prosecutor is empty. He has been thrown out (Revelation 12:7-10).

Now imagine again that we are brought forward as the accused. Terrible punishment awaits us. But what a surprise for Christians. The chair of the prosecutor is empty! The prosecutor has not been admitted; he's finished.

That is why there will not be a hearing against the Christians. The accusations against them have been dropped. Jesus Christ has destroyed the business of the accuser. The devil may hate the followers of Jesus. On earth he may even destroy their lives, but in heaven his wicked game is finished. He prefers not even to appear in God's courtroom.

Through his death Jesus provided an entirely new legal basis. He himself was placed on the defense, was in fact condemned to death because our guilt was placed on him. But when the executioner came to lead him away into eternal hell he was told that the accused was innocent. There was no fault in Jesus. The executioner had to release his victim.

And now the real judgment scene is a closed matter for

all genuine Christians. It is finished. No time is wasted on that. "There is therefore now no condemnation for those who are in Christ Jesus" (Romans 8:1). One could still have court proceedings against them. But it's a foregone conclusion that everyone would be acquitted, as if they had never done anything wrong, never had done any evil. No fault would be found in them!

Imagine the catalog of sins in your own life. You know what all has happened. You know that you don't deserve to be acquitted. But you're told, "There is no accusation against you. It is all paid." Can anything be more important than that people accept this offer of Jesus' substitutionary punishment and claim it for themselves?

When we do that there is no need ever to dig up old guilt and debts. Unfortunately, this does happen. Even Christians warm up misdeeds that have been forgotten long ago. Once more they make them the basis of accusations. That is a very serious sin. It is also a sin to dig up one's own sin which has been forgiven long ago. The devil, that mean old liar, will try to do that again and again, especially with people who have a tender conscience and a wavering faith. He accuses them of never really having dealt with an old sin, or that new misdeeds have brought new condemnation. Because the devil can't do anything with God anymore, because his accusations fall on deaf ears, he tries to do it behind his back. He whispers into the ears of God's children that they are damned after all. Not even the blood of Jesus can save them now, he says.

We need not listen to that suggestion of the devil. Since Jesus died on the cross God's people cannot be condemned. Let us cling to that glorious truth as long as we live. Let us actually do what we so often sing,

Rock of Ages, cleft for me,
Let me hide myself in Thee;
Let the water and the blood,
From Thy riven side which flowed,
Be of sin the double cure;
Cleanse me from its guilt and pow'r.

CHAPTER SIX

TOO GOOD TO BE TRUE?

All kinds of theories are spread nowadays about dying and what comes after death. Thick books are written about it and they sell well. But let's be careful! A lot of nonsense is being said and printed.

Should we not rather consult the Bible, the eternal word of truth? But unfortunately even here we have to watch, because not everything that claims to be biblical truth is healthy biblical teaching. One has to learn to really understand the meaning of the biblical texts. One needs to know the larger connections, to read Scripture within its context, or else there is the danger of wrong interpretation of individual verses.

Sometimes when people pronounce their pious ideas I feel like withdrawing into a quiet place and asking: "O Lord, what does it really mean? Is their theory correct? Are you really backing them up in what they teach as your servants?" I'm certain that much of it is not true. Frequently God would likely say, "Oh, you ignorant people! You just don't know any better. You have misunderstood me completely. It is really quite different, because I am different from the way you imagine me."

Obviously with some questions this is not as serious as with others. We discover later that we were mistaken, but it has no further serious consequences.

On the other hand, some questions are too urgent, too hot, to leave them unanswered. If some say, "Death ends everything," and others insist, "There is a life after death and a judgment for all people," can one shrug one's shoulders and think, "Oh, well, let's wait and see"? If it is true, as Christians say it is, that after death there comes the judgment, should one not know what one's chances are? Christians also insist—and they do this on the basis of Scripture—that one who believes in Jesus Christ need not fear the judgment because he has already been acquitted.

That would be wonderful. Almost too good to be true. But, is it really true? Isn't that a calculation that has been made apart from God, our stern judge? No, it really is true! The resurrection of Jesus is proof of that.

In Romans 4:25 we read that Jesus was raised for our justification. When Jesus was taken from the grave, God took a position on the matter of our guilt and Jesus' substitution for it. Had God not agreed to Jesus paying with his death on the cross for our sins, he would have left him in the grave. The attempted redemption would have failed. Our guilt would continue to be upon us and the devil would naturally have the right to condemn us. Paul writes to the Corinthians: "If Christ has not been raised, your faith is futile and you are still in your sins" (1 Corinthians 15:17).

However, because God said yes to the substitutionary death of Jesus, because he confirmed the innocence of his beloved son, he could not leave him in death. Because of the resurrection of Jesus Christ it is not presumptuous for me to say, "My sins are blotted out. There is no need to talk about them anymore."

The devil, that old liar, doesn't want to acknowledge this. Again and again he comes with his old tricks and whispers, "Maybe salvation is not valid for you. Maybe you should make some contribution yourself. Perhaps this one sin is not covered by God's forgiveness. Perhaps salvation is too cheap to really cover all your sins."

Peter had been a witness to the death and resurrection of Jesus. At first he also had difficulty believing in the resurrection. But when he thought more deeply about all the experiences that he had had with Jesus, he affirmed with great feeling that there was no other possibility! It was impossible that Jesus should have remained in death (Acts 2:24). Jesus, a corpse, decaying in the grave forever? Unthinkable! Not Jesus. He was infinitely stronger than death. When he came out of the grave the most conclusive evidence had been provided for the fact that the devil's game was over. He had lost.

Since that Easter in Jerusalem death looks very different. Of course, the devil still wants to scare us. He still has a little room left in which to maneuver, but he is powerless to change the basic facts. He still threatens and shakes his fist. Now and then he may even strike us a severe blow. We may suffer painful injuries, but he cannot destroy us. Nor will he ever be able to bring us into judgment and condemnation. His accusations are not accepted as valid anymore, because through Jesus Christ they have become worthless.

Now the fear of death disappears. If we come to crossroads, we no longer need to choose the wrong road because we are afraid. Now we dare choose the right road even if it leads to suffering and death.

Dying is still not child's play, but death no longer scares us away from obedience. It is wonderful to live with Jesus and to serve him, but if suddenly the call to death comes, we don't need to be afraid, because as Christians we know the best is yet to be.

The apostle Paul asked himself once, "What is better, to continue living or to die?" Finally he was able to write to the congregation at Philippi, "My desire is to depart and be with Christ. . . . But to remain in the flesh is more necessary on your account" (Philippians 1:23-24).

Possibly some people also have to continue living here on earth not for the sake of others, but for their own sake. Some dear sick people have a hard time believing that. They would like to die. There is nothing more that they can do in this life, and they suffer great pain. But God does not call them home yet for whatever reason he may have.

We have no demands to make on God, no instructions to give to him. Whether he calls us home today or tomorrow, whether with or without pain, one thing is certain: He will deliver our soul from death (Psalm 33:19). God will not leave us in death. That is our assurance and comfort.

Let us think once again about the courtroom into which we are to be led as the accused. The sinister prosecutor is not there anymore. That is a miracle. Another miracle is that Jesus is our defense and our judge at the same time. The whole trial has been placed in his hands. He is our best friend. He demonstrated that when he gave his life for us.

I have witnessed court trials in which the defense did a miserable job. One could feel it that the case didn't really interest him. If he had wanted to, he could have achieved a much more favorable verdict. And judges too sometimes make a rather questionable impression. They may already have decided to condemn the accused even before they have heard all the evidence.

But in our case Jesus himself is going to be our defense and judge in the last judgment. There is no question whatsoever that he is going to acquit us. If our best friend is also our judge, what can go wrong? Who is going to condemn the one that Christ has set free (Romans 8:33)? Our judgment has already taken place; the verdict was carried out on Jesus. That is the kind of Savior we have. That takes the sting and fear out of dying. Even the last bit of the difficult road now will work to our advantage. Death itself will open the door for us into the other world, into life eternal.

CHAPTER SEVEN

AS WE LIVE, SO WE DIE

We have considered in previous chapters the inevitability of death and the faith-building and encouraging prospects beyond the grave. Now let us explore concrete ways to prepare ourselves for dying.

Before me is a booklet, *The Art of Dying*, by Albert Mauder. Let me quote a few sentences:

> Whether we die easily or with difficulty, reconciled or unreconciled, whether we die after severe struggle or in serene peace, that is not something that is decided when our final hour comes. That is something that has been decided through the years, through a long period of preparation. It is decided by our lifestyle. Our dying is predetermined by our living, and our entire life is a preparation for our dying. It isn't as if somewhere, sometime there's a radical change, a change which in contrast to our normal life, suddenly starts us on the road to dying. Indeed not. Our life changes imperceptibly into dying. To be precise, we start to die at the moment when we begin consciously to really live. Our entire life is a life towards death. That is why generally everyone dies more or less the way he lived. For that reason, the beginning of assistance and counsel for dying has to be precise instruction for right living. It is impossible to separate the one from the other.

We're going to die the way we have lived. Exceptions simply prove the rule. There are many examples of wonderfully spiritual people who had a difficult time dying. Those who knew them expected that their death would be a beautiful, peaceful departure into glory. But instead it was a dreadful and dark experience. Let us not be too hasty and say that it became clear that the person's whole life had been hypocritical, that at last the truth came out. None of us knows in advance how we are going to die.

I know about faithful servants of God whose lives were eloquent proof of the fact that God had used them as servants in his vineyard, but before they died they passed through periods of severe depression, doubt, and temptation. It would appear that God had to lead these persons through a painful experience of purification, to remove from them all that was of self, before he could cover them with white clothes of justification.

Nevertheless, what Albert Mauder says is true: "Our entire life is a preparation for dying." A wise person once said, "Live every day the way you will wish on the last day of your life that you had lived." Live so that you prepare for yourself a good dying experience.

Jesus told about a man who apparently realized only after his death that he had not lived right (Luke 16:19-'23). Morally he didn't seem to have been a bad man, and yet he suddenly found himself in hell. It appears that he was surprised, as if an injustice had been done to him because he had not been warned.

We have a similar case in Luke 12:20. That is the story about the successful farmer who thought only about his good crops and bigger barns, but not about his soul. Not until the time for dying came did he realize that he had neglected to take care of his eternal destiny.

On another occasion Jesus talked about people who actually had done great deeds in his name. But they too had to recognize in the end that their heroic deeds were worthless because they neglected to do the will of God (Matthew 7:21-23). I'm afraid that's going to be the experience of many people. Not until just before they die, or even afterwards, will they realize that their life missed its goal—that they blew it.

Those who would take the long view in preparing themselves for dying may profitably search the Bible to find out what it has to say about this. And it's all there, and not complicated at all. Two steps describe it:

1. *Make a clear decision for Jesus Christ!* Our salvation depends only on one thing, our belonging to Jesus. Sometime, somewhere that will have to be definitely established, and not only from our side but also from the side of Jesus Christ, so that he himself will say: "I know this person. He belongs to me. No one can snatch him out of my hand." That is important and decisive. This strong connection to Jesus is described in the Bible in vivid pictures: Our names are written in his book—a seal is placed on our forehead—we are as much part of him as the branches are part of the vine—he lives in our hearts—we are his sheep.

If only we would recognize once and for all that only those people will go to heaven whom Jesus recognizes as his own people. The Bible speaks with frightening earnestness about people who thought they were in the good graces of God and who simply would not believe the fact that Jesus never knew them.

If Jesus says, "This person is a part of me," there is nothing further to clarify. Then we will be with him in all eternity. But if he doesn't say that, we may weep or rave and insist that the opposite is true, but it will do no good. You can present your church membership card, your baptism certificate proving that you have been a church member for 50 years, that you have contributed liberally to the support of the church, that you have regularly attended worship services. Of course, all these things have their merit, but they are worthless in the matter of securing your salvation. Your name has to be written in the Book of Life. That's the only thing that matters. That's not an idea I thought up. Jesus himself said it clearly many times.

Now because that is so, permit me to ask you personally and directly, "How is it with you? Is your name written in the Book of Life in which all the names of those who belong to Jesus are recorded? Or have you not even seriously thought about that?" If such is the case, then I wish for you no peace until this question is settled. Indeed, I beg you earnestly, make Jesus Christ the Lord of your life. Why not tell him quite simply: "Lord Jesus, from now on I want to belong to you. Write my name into your book. From now on tell me what I must do."

Many persons have grown up in Christian surroundings and sort of slithered along spiritually through the years. If you ask them, "Do you belong to Jesus? Have you made a decision? Do you know that he has accepted you?" they give no clear answer. I'm surprised and shocked at how many young Christians apparently don't know whether they belong to Jesus or not.

In a German Christmas hymn we sing, "If Jesus had been born a thousand times in Bethlehem but not in you, you would still be lost to all eternity."

Why don't you settle this matter of belonging to Jesus? He made it very clear who belongs to him: "Every one who acknowledges me before men, I also will acknowledge before my Father who is in heaven" (Matthew 10:32). If we do not confess Christ in our immediate surroundings, we simply show that we are not clear in this matter. With the first Christians it was relatively simple; those who believed in Jesus stepped forward and were baptized. That is still right and proper today. In any event, the new convert has to tell family, colleagues, and friends that he or she has made a decision for Jesus.

That the decision for Jesus will need to be confirmed by a lifetime of words and deeds is something else. The Bible calls that sanctification. Without that even a conversion remains worthless. That is why the second important instruction on the road to real living is:

2. *Be serious about your sanctification.* Without sanctification no one will see God, says the Bible. Sanctification is the result of a genuine decision for Christ. The fact that we belong to Jesus must be seen in all areas of our life. Some things we notice very quickly ourselves, and through the power of Christ we break with old sins and habits. The old lifestyle is discarded the way one takes off an old garment.

In some areas, however, it is more difficult than that. If people around us see nothing bad in a certain matter, if all of them do it, then it is possible that we may continue doing wrong for a long time without even noticing it. The apostles frequently had to warn young Christians who lived in big cities to stop living after the fashion of their environment. Stop lying. Don't steal, but work. Avoid immorality. Honor your marriage. Lead a quiet, peaceable life. Forgive each other. Love each other. Stop hating and quarreling. Cast off sin, your old nature. No sin will go with us into heaven. Nothing unclean may enter there.

Following casting off such things, we still need constant cleansing. Although we are serious about following Jesus, about our discipleship, it is possible to be overtaken unsuspectedly by sin. The old nature can so easily break through and assert itself again. That which we had conquered once asserts itself again to conquer us. A little "white lie" or an unkind word may quickly have been spoken in an unguarded moment. Anger may have suddenly overtaken me, or fear made me a coward. Things like that have to be taken care of right away; immediate cleansing is necessary. We cannot afford to live with guilt that has not been removed. It is possible that suddenly there is no time for straightening things out. Unfortunately, there are more examples than we need of this.

A son left his family without saying good-bye. Because his father had been harsh with him and wouldn't give him what he wanted, he slammed the door and drove off. A half hour later he was brought home dead. There had been no time for reconciliation.

Don't take this matter lightly. Be reconciled with your opponent, your family, while you still have the possibility to do this. Tomorrow it could be too late. I know that we need to add "as much as it is in my power." We must always be ready to extend the hand of peace, but it would be a miserable peace if it were gained at the cost of truth.

Those who are serious about their sanctification also accept God's correction. God is faithful. He will not let us get onto a wrong road without warning. He does not watch dispassionately as we plunge into disaster. Of course, some people want to accuse God of not having warned them. The rich man in hell begged for Lazarus to leave heaven and go to his five brothers to warn them. And what was the answer? "They have Moses and the prophets. . . . If they do not hear [them], neither will they be convinced if some one should rise from the dead" (Luke 16:29-31). They have been warned all right. If they don't heed the warnings which they have, they will also land in hell.

God gives sensitive and effective warning signals. At first he beckons mildly and gently—after that sometimes with a loud and hard voice. Some people will face a rude awakening when God recounts for them how clearly he has warned them. If we pay no attention to the caution sign at the crossroads but instead step on the gas, it is a foregone conclusion that sooner or later we're going to have an accident. In that case, however, we shouldn't blame the police.

We should never blame God when we land in a catastrophic mess. Nor is every accident or catastrophe the result of personal fault. We see this clearly in the case of Job, and Jesus explains the same point in John 9:3. Sometimes when God leads his children into trials his ways are too mysterious for us to understand. We should be startled when we are struck by a heavy blow and ask ourselves, "What is God trying to tell me? Why does he have to talk so painfully loud? Is it possible that I did not heed earlier warnings?"

The apostle Peter too needed godly correction more than once. For example, he was so caught up in his Jewish way of thinking that he was not ready to preach and eat in the house of a Roman officer. God had to really put his servant Peter in his place so that he wouldn't say no where God had said yes. Later, too, as a leader of the church, he had to learn to change some of his thinking. Old and basic articles of faith which he had observed since his youth had to be discarded. It is really wonderful when Spirit-filled and seasoned servants in God's kingdom show a readiness to change their attitude and switch to new thinking and walking new roads when God clearly calls them to do so.

Another point that is important for everyone who takes holiness seriously is the need to pay attention to the right priorities. Priority means the sequence of important things. What comes first? Which of two things is more important? Jesus made crystal clear that the kingdom of God must always be first. If we keep that in mind and do it, he will take care of everything else. He specifically promised that in Matthew 6:33.

But here's a man who first wants to bury his father before he follows Jesus. Isn't it the most elementary duty of a son to see that his father gets a decent burial? Jesus said, "No. Leave that to others. Something else is more important. Follow me" (Matthew 8:22).

Those who want to be faithful to Jesus dare not let society dictate to them which things are most important. Isn't that an area where we often are too cowardly? We know very well what things should have priority but we are afraid we're going to upset some people if we behave differently. We allow business or politics to dictate our priorities. Sometimes we comfort ourselves and say: "Oh, well, the situation doesn't really suit me. But for the time being I'll accept it in order not to make waves. Later, if there's an opportunity, I'll try to change things. Then first things will again be first, the way they should be."

But can anything, even temporarily and for a short time, be more important than the kingdom of God! And what are we to do in the midst of all this compromise when suddenly we remember that we have to die?

If we were in charge of our time, and if we knew that

we definitely had a certain number of years at our disposal, then we could divide our time according to our own pleasure. Likely we would place the most important things somewhat towards the end, perhaps in fourth or fifth place. Naturally we would allow the most time for them in order to convince ourselves at least that we do have the right value judgments. But what happens if God calls a halt to our life before we get to the most important things? What will we do if there is no tomorrow for us? We will never get to point four even though we knew this was the most important of all.

If we actually knew how little time there is left for us, wouldn't we arrange our priorities differently?

I heard of a famous person who for many years was an enthusiastic golfer. One day he suddenly stopped playing. A friend asked him why. The man said, "I'm now 50 years old. If all goes well, I might still have another 20 years to do something worthwhile, something that will last. I don't want to waste these few remaining years playing golf."

Sports and play can be necessary recreation. And yet when we think about dying, when we consider that perhaps we have only a little time left, then we will want to calculate wisely, always putting the kingdom of God first.

CHAPTER EIGHT

STRANGERS AND PILGRIMS

How shall I aportion my life, considering the fact that perhaps I will need to die soon? What must I do so that in the last hour I will not be filled with remorse?

The Bible admonishes us to "serve the Lord with gladness" (Psalm 100:2). It tells us, "Never flag in zeal, be aglow with the Spirit, serve the Lord" (Romans 12:11). The king told his servants: "Trade until I return." And when he came back he punished the lazy servant severely (Luke 19:13-24). If we are serious about our sanctification we cannot arrange our life the way we please with a little bit of time and money here and there for the service of our Lord.

"Service is a lifestyle," my friend Peter J. Dyck insists. Christians are always in the service of their Lord, even when they take time out to eat or go on vacation. We are not responsible for all the work in the kingdom of our Lord. We cannot evangelize the whole world in five or ten years. Jesus simply expects us to do our part. We can work without getting nervous even if there is little time. We do not have to fill a certain quota before we are called home. But what if he returns before you have completed your task? Never mind. Just keep at it so that he will not find you idly loafing around, but working.

As a young recruit in the army I was allowed to stay behind once while my comrades went out to do some rather difficult exercises. An infection in my leg had made it impossible for me to participate in the strenuous march. As soon as the soldiers had gone, I promptly lay down and fell asleep. But I made a serious miscalculation. Suddenly the captain stood in front of me. You can imagine the scene that followed: "Aren't you ashamed of yourself?" he shouted. "Your comrades are crawling on their bellies through dirt and you haven't even swept the barracks! If I had found you at least with a broom in your hand, I would have said nothing." I had to admit he was right. Even if I had not finished the work, I should have at least started it.

When Jesus returns, when he calls us home, the work doesn't need to be finished, but he should at least find us with a "broom in our hands." You know what I mean. In Asia, Africa, and Latin America our brothers and sisters are fighting at the front. They struggle, sweat, and bleed. In our large cities evangelists are struggling in slums against crime, drugs, and vice of every description. They give their last strength to save at least some. How can we then sit back, relax, and simply do nothing or only what happens to please us?

In this life we never have enough time. Soon the tools will be taken from our hands. We will stop working. Someone else will take over. Then we can do no more. May the Lord at his coming at least find us active.

You older brothers and sisters, you who don't have the strength anymore to work. Now you have more time to pray. Have you consciously included that in your daily routine? So many are fully occupied with all kinds of interesting hobbies, and suddenly it is evening and they have had no time for prayer.

Those who prepare long-range for their dying, those who are serious about their salvation, must never forget that they are strangers here on earth. Dying comes easier if we are not too much at home here. "For here we have no lasting city, but we seek the city which is to come" (Hebrews 13:14). Peter refers to Christians as aliens and exiles in this world (1 Peter 2:11). The old patriarchs of the faith lived in movable tents. All their life they were nomads, wanderers, strangers who were merely tolerated by their neighbors. And we Christians? Have we not settled down, made ourselves comfortable, and become adjusted to our society? To be sure we know a few lovely songs about our home in heaven. And we like to sing them too. But in reality we are comfortable in this world and heaven is a strange place for us. One song some of us sing includes the words,

> Our earthly homes are perfected
> While our eternal home is neglected.

Many a wealthy Christian builds himself a luxurious home in old age, which he has to vacate before the paint is really dry. Can we do that if we are merely strangers in a world where innumerable refugees do not even have a roof over their heads?

If we consciously accept and endorse our pilgrimage status, we also need to be careful that we do not become entangled socially, economically, and politically with the affairs of this world in a way that will make our disengagement impossible. Sometimes I fear for Christians who seem to have sold themselves to this world. They could not extricate themselves again, even if they tried. We dare not become captive to our houses, our business, our associations and clubs, our friendships and relatives. They dare not keep us back when our Lord wants us to move foreward.

Before entering new commitments we should always ask whether these new commitments are in harmony with our pilgrim status. We will not be able to stay here. The visible world will disappear. Only the invisible world is eternal. I know that the Bible also says, "Seek the welfare of the city where I have sent you" (Jeremiah 29:7). And some Christians need to be admonished to take part in the social, economic, and political movements of their society, to strive for more justice in public life. This is part of our task, and is important. But we still need to keep our priorities straight, and see these other pursuits in the light of eternity, in the light of our number one task. Then they will always be priority number two.

On the other hand, because we are strangers and pilgrims, we will need to expect that the world will push us to the edge. They may even hate and persecute us. We shouldn't mind too much if the world lets us know that we're not wanted. Jesus taught us that and has given us the model.

If there is danger that we become too much at home in this world, then God may have to lead us into painful experiences to remind us where we really belong.

A bitter disappointment, a heavy loss, perhaps an illness that brings us to the brink of death are all means by which God can loosen the bonds with which we are tied to the world. My uncle buried three of his grown children within a year, the last one his youngest child, only 26 years old. When the pastor expressed his condolences my uncle replied: "One more cord cut that holds me down, and one more cord tied that pulls me up."

It is mighty painful when God starts cutting the cords that tie us to this earth. But we must continue our pilgrimage until he calls us too at last: "Come home now! It's time to stop your sojourn in a strange land."

PRACTICAL MATTERS

Once my father came home from visiting a young man who was dying. He told us that the young man had given him a serious warning which he was to pass on to the people at his funeral: "Tell them to get ready before they are seriously ill. Once you are as weak as I am now, you can't take care of anything anymore, no matter how important it is."

We have said that all our life we should be prepared for our dying. Now, however, we mention a few practical things which need to be taken care of as we near the end of life. These things demand our attention when we are still strong enough physically and mentally to deal with them, not at the end of life.

One day the prophet Isaiah came to King Hezekiah to tell him, "Set your house in order; for you shall die" (Isaiah 38:1). That was a clear call from God to a man who was up to his ears in important work. Jesus said, "Do not lay up for yourselves treasures on earth, where moth and rust consume.... For where your treasure is, there will your heart be also" (Matthew 6:19-21). When we notice that the end seems to be coming closer, we have all the more reason to let go of earthly things and to focus our heart on heavenly things. Job comforted himself by observing that he came into the world naked and would leave it naked (Job 1:21). In Switzerland we have a saying: "The clothes of the deceased don't have pockets. You brought nothing into the world; you won't take anything with you."

Because that is so, we should not try to get rich. If, however, we do prosper financially, we need to be doubly careful not to become miserly and greedy.

I know a Christian farmer who had a large farm with 70 thoroughbred horses. During the war he became a refugee and had to abandon his beautiful farm. On foot, and with nothing but a small handbag, he started on his way. He never once looked back.

To separate yourself from worldly goods is one of the absolute necessities in the preparation for dying. Let me quote once more Albert Mauder and his book, *The Art of Dying:*

> In the course of life our treasures just happen to accumulate. Most of it is worthless stuff. Anyone who has had to liquidate a household can sing a song about that. Most of the things that seem so important to us which we have difficulty parting with become worthless even during our own lifetime as they are eaten by moth or rust. Why do we burden ourselves with it? Here is someone who still has his wedding suit in his closet even though he has gained 30 pounds. There is a 60-year-old who still has her childhood doll. Another is unable to recycle his schoolbooks, and still someone else just cannot part with his faded and yellow pictures.
>
> Learning to die starts with tossing away and recycling, with getting rid of all that stuff that is basically nothing more than ballast and junk. It is a good and spiritual exercise, worthy to be copied, to regularly, every five years have a massive raid in your house to get rid of

everything that you don't need anymore. That requires courage and discipline. Look carefully at all your "treasures" and then imagine that after your death your relatives have to sort it all out and get rid of it. That is sobering and helps you to toss and recycle things. Garbage men are patient, and for other things there are telephone numbers in the book of agencies who know what to do with it.

Now that's pretty strong language, don't you think? But isn't Albert Mauder right? As painful as it may be, we have to learn to "clear the decks" from time to time. People who upon retirement move from a large home into a small apartment or into an old people's home know how painful it is to let go of almost everything because there is no room where they are going.

Perhaps it is possible to give away a few especially lovely things instead of throwing them away. But what shall we give away? Mauder thinks that books, dishes, jewelry, and perhaps a few pieces of beautiful furniture could be given away to make someone happy. But if in doubt whether our gift would make our friends or relatives happy, it would be best simply to discard them without regret or bitterness.

In giving things away we actually give a bit of our heart away. That is not easy, but we have to be hard with ourselves and start the process while we still have the strength to do it. We should not merely give away things that we won't miss anyway, but actually everything that we can spare. Naturally we shouldn't give away things that we still need, but it is surprising how little we really need when we have become old and stiff.

Certainly we can resist greedy would-be heirs who already during our lifetime want to "relieve" us of our possessions. Sometimes even the darling children and grandchildren come and say, "Mother or Grandma, you don't really need that anymore. I would be glad for it." In cases like that it's perfectly okay to say, "Not so fast, my dear. I happen to still be alive and I can use these things quite well myself."

Good preparation for dying also requires a last will and testament. Albert Mauder thinks that at 50 years of age everybody should have one. Most likely he's right. We should write or have someone else write our last will and testament early, making it clear and precise, and of course keeping in mind legal requirements. It is shocking to see how many families get into arguments and quarrels because the parents or an uncle or aunt neglected to spell out clearly their last wishes in a legal document or because they failed to take into account certain mandatory legal demands.

Those who administer homes for the aged know how scandalous the behavior can be when lonely old people close their eyes for the last time. Before that their loving relatives hardly ever visited them. But scarcely have they taken the last breath than the relatives are on the spot. Sometimes valuable jewelry or certain papers that might prove to be embarrassing disappear while the deceased relative is still in the room. It is therefore absolutely necessary as part of the preparation for dying to have a last will and testament, and to make sure that it is in a safe place.

With our last resources we should, of course, provide first for those persons for whom we are responsible. Those who fail to do that are worse than the heathen, the Bible tells us in 1 Timothy 5:8. We must protect our marriage partner so that after our death greedy heirs cannot outsmart and rob him or her. If we do not feel competent in this sort of thing, we should seek counsel from a pastor or from some other knowledgeable and trustworthy person who can help us take care of all the details in a proper and legal way.

I have frequently observed how spiritually minded people definitely planned to leave a portion of their inheritance to the church or to missions. However, they failed to include this in their last will and testament, and after their death the heirs disregarded that wish.

"So teach us to number our days, that we may get a heart of wisdom" is what the Bible teaches. Part of that is to let go in good time of our possessions and to dispose of the rest in such a way that God is honored by it and quarrels are avoided.

CHAPTER TEN

LEARNING TO LET GO

As Christians it is our duty and privilege in everything that we do to honor our Lord Jesus Christ. In all situations of life we are required to look for a solution which pleases him and which furthers the building of the kingdom and the welfare of people. That is why we should avoid making decisions that would embarrass our relatives after our death, or perhaps even make them angry and thus unwittingly bring disgrace upon our Lord.

How quickly such things can happen. A fine and spiritual mother who had many children and grandchildren lived and worked on a large farm. She was fully in charge. She was a wise woman, respected by everyone. When she fell ill her children and grandchildren frequently came to visit her. Everyone in the community praised the absolutely exemplary harmony that was so clearly evident in this large family. After the mother had died, the heirs began to ask themselves what should happen to the farm. Then they discovered to their dismay that shortly before their mother died, she had willed the farm to the youngest son at an exceptionally low price. This had been done without consulting the other children. It's not surprising that tensions and a bitter family quarrel arose almost immediately after the funeral.

It is of the utmost importance as one gets older to place responsibilities into the hands of some other competent person. This is a first step, a necessary preparation for dying, even if the end is still not in sight. Our successors have to be appointed in good time, and everything must be taken care of decently and in order. Sooner or later we have to do it. We do well to begin the process early, even if it is a painful and complicated matter.

"He must increase but I must decrease" is also valid in our occupation. Some good Christian people cling so long to their office or position that one must assume they think they are the only ones who can do it. The consequence is, of course, that even among Christians terrible things happen simply because an older person neglected to talk in good time about the future of the business, and the orderly procedure for a transfer or a successor. We too easily delay because we see this as a difficult matter. We are afraid it will lead to tension. We know that not everyone concerned is really spiritually minded and selfless. So we simply avoid the ticklish topic, or else discuss it only with those who agree with us.

Unfortunately, close relatives often are unable to deal objectively with each other in such situations. They don't want to hurt each other, but under no circumstances do they want to be short-changed either. If, in such a situation, a good solution cannot be arrived at by everyone, then we need to search together for another solution or ask a wise brother or sister to arbitrate. It simply must not happen that Christians in situations like that run to a lawyer or part unreconciled. Jesus is the great reconciler. How can we tolerate the prospect of people quarreling over our miserable possessions? In matters of money and property it is necessary, to prevent this from happening, to take things into our own hands in good time.

Such a transfer is not always possible without friction. It can be painful to give up a business one has built up over the years with great effort. And yet the time comes in our life when we must let go and make room for others. It is wholesome to relinquish one's hold on worldly possessions. And once the business has been transferred, the secret is to keep your mouth shut and speak only when asked. If young people turn a few things upside down, then so be it; they have the right to make their own mistakes.

Those who systematically prepare to die should also gradually relinquish responsibilities in church and society. One needs to write out one's resignation and lay down one office after the other. If the job is a particularly difficult one, it is all the more necessary to gradually groom and prepare someone else over a period of time. Sometimes it is possible for a while to work along as the number two man before completely resigning.

An experienced man of God said once, "If you are healthy you can keep increasing your work load until the age of 50; but after 50 you should write a resignation every two or three years." If the shifting of responsibilities is done gradually, the work need not suffer. Don't wait until people give you a more or less direct hint. Step back, even if others think it is too early, and don't let them change your mind. You can always pitch in to help out if necessary.

It is essential, of course, that before we leave, our successors are thoroughly initiated and oriented so that they are ready for the task. We should not be so proud as to keep all the knowledge to ourselves and then secretly rejoice when we see our successor make all the mistakes.

Some personal matters we may continue to take care of for quite a while. We may take care of our little property, paying the insurance premiums and taxes ourselves. We may even negotiate new agreements, but in light of preparing for death it is advisable to have at least one knowledgeable person know all about our dealings. It can be embarrassing and problematic if a person suddenly dies and no one knows where his documents are, and which commitments have been made. Even within the family it is advisable in financial matters to draw up an agreement and have it signed by all parties concerned.

But what shall you do if suddenly it is too late to draw up a long agreement on paper? If possible, invite two impartial witnesses in and give them an oral declaration. If only one person is involved in carrying out one's last wishes, and especially if that person is one of the people directly affected, then that can easily cause distrust and bitterness.

Unfortunately, the good businessman in the family is frequently the one who is appointed as the executor. If it happens that the inheritance is smaller than expected or that there is an aura of secretness about the affair, then one can expect the others to feel that there has been deception. There seems to be ground for suspicion, but of course nobody wants to fight. Nevertheless, the love relationship has been strained. And the only reason for that is because somebody didn't prepare his dying wisely enough.

It is one of the duties of a Christian to manage financial affairs carefully. That is why these things should be taken care of while our minds are still functioning well. It is essential to remember that certain agreements may elapse after a few years. Possibly at one time you informed your loved ones of your wishes for distributing your property, but things may have changed and what was said is no longer valid. A sum of money has been repaid, for instance, or someone is in an entirely new situation. In such cases, these things have to be discussed again. When my wife and I went abroad a few years ago, we informed one of our sons about all our "business." If we had died in an accident he would have known precisely what to do. Recently I had that paper in my hand again and was surprised to see how much of it no longer was applicable. I had to reorient my son to my current affairs.

Persons who have problems with paperwork have a double reason to invite a friend or expert to help them get all these mundane details taken care of in good time.

Many of us say we would never participate in a war. As followers of Jesus we are children of peace. That's great! But this peace position should also be demonstrated in a sober and practical manner right here in our immediate neighborhood and in our extended family by doing everything in our power to prevent any cause for disagreement, tension, and quarrels. The way we settle our earthly affairs should leave no room for tension and disagreements after we have passed on.

CHAPTER ELEVEN

THE LAST HOURS

I said in the last chapter that cleaning up our affairs, getting rid of a lot of unnecessary stuff in our house, is a necessary step in the preparation for dying. Now there is another inward and spiritual cleaning up process that also needs to be taken care of in preparation for death.

The best method is to constantly clean up all guilt as we go along. Since we never know when our last hour will come, and whether or not we will then have time to clear up an old affair that is still on our conscience, we should continuously talk things over with God, and as much as necessary with people also. If we cannot handle some of these matters alone, we should find a pastor or a spiritual counselor who can help us clear things up.

Unfortunately, many people carry with them a heavy burden all their life, some dark secret which troubles their conscience.

Just two brief examples. A good woman, mother of many children, suddenly realized she would be dying soon. In fact, she had only a few days left to live. Only then did she confess to her husband that he was not the father of their oldest son, by now a full-grown man and married. For more than twenty years she had kept her adultery secret.

A man was dying in the beautiful house that he had built for himself. He confessed that years before he had burned down his old house to collect the insurance money. He had burned it down during a heavy thunderstorm, and everyone simply thought that lightning had struck it.

Likely not many of us are carrying a burden this heavy, but still there may be a lingering grudge that troubles us, or the hatred of a person who wronged us that keeps bothering us. A young woman said: "When my brother opens the door, I get goose bumps. When I was a girl of 13 he raped me. He destroyed something in me. I hate my brother. I cannot forgive him."

Oh, the conflict that emerges in our immediate relationships. How much injustice is unleashed between husband and wife, parent and children, colleagues and neighbors! Perhaps at the time of conversion we drew a line through all this. It seemed all forgiven by God. But now, at the approach of death, the old wound is opened again, the old hatred, the guilt, and the sins that were never confessed—all accuse us. Earlier the whole thing didn't seem that important. It only bothered us a little now and then. But now it is the cause of sleepless nights. If so, why not simply muster all your courage and take care of the matter once and for all while you still are able to do so? Either pay the appropriate person a visit or invite him to come and see you for a private and confidential talk. Perhaps the other person doesn't even suspect that something is wrong, or else has long ago forgotten it. But on your conscience it has left a dark spot and that must be removed before you are ready to die.

Perhaps it isn't even guilt that needs to be confessed, but a spiritual concern that needs to be talked over. You may feel the need to pass on to your family, neighbor, or church some observation, a concern, or a wish.

An old woman invited her pastor to her bedside and said, "It seems to me in our congregation there is no preaching anymore about the wrath of God. Brother, don't keep the seriousness of God's wrath from the people." These words, spoken by a dying woman, made a deep impression on that minister.

It is possible that in the last hours we are especially burdened for a certain person, perhaps an unbelieving or sick member of the family. In this, too, Jesus is our example. Looking down from the cross he saw his mother whom he needed to leave behind. As the oldest son he had probably assumed the major responsibility for the maintenance of the family. Now he told his disciple John, "Please take care of my mother." Dying can become even more difficult when you have to leave behind a person you love but who may be frail, or otherwise unable to deal with the affairs of life. In such a case it is absolutely right to request a trustworthy person to assume responsibility for the loved one.

At the same time, I must urgently warn you not to use the last hour of dying for emotional extortions. When our loved ones are filled with the pain of saying their final good-byes, we dare not ask them to make promises that they simply cannot keep. We dare not request them to say yes to something to which they would have said no when they were not so worked up emotionally. Mothers have ruined the lives of children by getting them to make a solemn promise just before she died. We should be very careful not to misuse the deathbed for the fulfillment of personal wishes, no matter how well meaning those desires may be.

To work through last and final concerns can require all our physical, mental, and spiritual resources. This is all the more reason not to wait until that energy is gone. There are problems that need more than ten minutes to clear up. Start early enough. To get ready for dying means to let go of things of this world, to let go of people we love, of ideas we have, and to become free at last for the big journey.

CHAPTER TWELVE

GRATITUDE DISPELS BITTERNESS

All those practical things we talked about in the earlier chapters can become disturbing and difficult for us. It is therefore of utmost importance to have the right attitude. While we are in the process of winding down, constantly able to do less and have less, it is important that we learn to be thankful. Learning to give thanks for all the good things we have received and for what we still have is a great blessing. Only that will spare us from becoming bitter.

We can give thanks for many delightful years which we were privileged to live together. We can appreciate our children and the joy of grandchildren. We can give thanks for the tasks which we were able to perform, for the people who crossed our path, for the church that has meant so much to us. As we look back in gratitude, we receive strength to give thanks for that which is still left: that we can still see and hear, that we can still go out on the street or porch, that we can still sit in our wheelchair, or watch the cherry blossoms from our bed. As the familiar song suggests, "Count your many blessings; count them one by one."

This is an essential exercise on the road to dying—learning to thank God for everything we still have, including the people who serve us, even though they don't do everything quite the way we would like them to do it. As long as we are still able, perhaps we should write a few letters of appreciation and encouragement to people who have meant a lot to us. And we should give our loved ones and those who take care of us grateful words and smiles as long as we are still able to do that. Here the difference becomes noticeable between Christians who are filled with the peace of God and for whom the expression of gratitude is a genuine desire and those people, Christians and non-Christians alike, who talk endlessly about their own accomplishments and how miserably they are now being treated by God and people.

Constant complaining simply makes us and those around us unhappy. On the other hand, a song of praise honors God and keeps our soul healthy. Of course, that needs to be practiced. It isn't something we can do just like that. We have to give ourselves a real push sometimes and say, "That's enough complaining. I want to praise the Lord as long as I live!" It's an open secret but true, that in this way we can continue to be useful for God even though our strength steadily diminishes.

By the way we live our old age we bring glory and honor to God. For young people we can become a shining example of the faithfulness of God.

CHAPTER THIRTEEN

HOW TO HANDLE A
DYING PERSON

It is likely that most of us before we die ourselves will be confronted with the death of someone else. Some of our loved ones, friends, and acquaintances will likely be called home before we are. To deal with the topic of dying would, therefore, be incomplete if we did not give some practical advice on how to handle dying people. There are helpful books today which explain the process of dying, the experience the dying person is going through, and how we can be of assistance. I have personally also had some experience, and can confirm what Albert Mauder and others say.

The process of dying (if it is not instantly caused by an accident or by heart failure) usually follows several phases which may not always be of the same duration or intensity, but in most cases are strikingly similar.

The first phase is the struggle to accept the fact that one is dying. The doctor, pastor, or loved ones have informed the patient that he is about to die. The patient has to know that. Fortunately, the conviction is growing that it is necessary to tell the patient the truth. Obviously, though, this truth needs to be transmitted in love and at the right time.

In facing the reality of imminent death, I believe that even in cases of incurable sickness we may ask God to do a miracle. I have experienced such miracles myself. If the patient wishes it, we should call the elders of the congregation and, as instructed in James 5:14-16, pray over him. At this point, however, I do not want to talk about faith healing, but only about the handling of the dying person. Even for the most spiritual believer the time will come when God will not answer his or her prayer for healing but will say, "Now it is your turn to come home."

To realize this is a shock for everyone. Even if we suspected it, now it is an irrevocable, indisputable fact. Some patients begin to shake or even suffer a heart attack. Even in cases where death had been anticipated and longed for this realization of the imminence of death is startling. But it is not true that the patient doesn't want to know the truth or cannot bear it. It is the healthy people who often don't have enough courage to talk about dying. It is a distinct advantage to have talked with the doctor and the pastor about the time and the manner of breaking the news. Some people are terribly clumsy in such things. Only true love finds the right words.

The first phase of being startled is usually followed by a phase of resistance. In the case of a Christian who is ready for death this may last only a few minutes, but it can also last days and weeks. It is possible that the dying one will blame God and denounce people. Sometimes the patient rages or cries or whimpers, begging for a prolongation of life, asking, "Why me? Why now?" A person can become quite impossible, and it requires an enormous amount of patience to see the dying one through this phase. He is

fighting with the last enemy, death (1 Corinthians 15:26).
Understanding that this is a common stage in the dying
process can be helpful.

This passionate defense can release in the patient all of
life's energies so that there is an upswing, and things look
more hopeful again. Indeed, it has happened that in the
intense inner struggle, the body is victorious over the sickness and the patient actually recovered again.

We should not blame the patient for his protest against
death. We should not think that if he were right with the
Lord he would have long ago wanted to depart and be
with him—and indeed should be glad for the final
release. Our struggle against death is simply an indication
of the fact that deep down we know that originally God
did not create us for death. Death is, and remains, un-
natural—something irrational. Consequently, every fiber
of our being protests against the clutching hand of the
grim reaper that is stretched out to get us.

Because the resistance struggle can actually cause a
temporary improvement in one's condition, the dying
person may deny that death is approaching. He is again
talkative and even jolly, interested in visitors and good
food. Some patients suddenly want to hear their favorite
music, or continue with their hobby. Some want to start
something new and quite impossible.

Now and then there are setbacks during this phase of
protesting against death. Occasionally one may hear re-
marks that are a clue to the fact that the patient is fooling
himself as well as his loved ones in order to hide the bitter
truth. On occasion it can prove difficult during this time
of optimism to keep the patient from doing senseless
things. But as far as possible, one should give the patient
freedom and fulfill his wishes. However, since it will be

necessary to curb the activity of the patient now and then, and since his strength is soon exhausted, this phase of confidence and self-deception usually does not last long.

Next the dying one is plunged into sadness and fear of death. He does not want to be alone. Frequently you have to hold his hand. He wants to see his loved ones once more. He takes leave of everything. Painfully he remembers many things that he will now lose. One should take time to sit at the bedside of the patient and let him talk once more about his life. It won't be necessary to say much yourself. Perhaps all that is necessary is to underscore the things that have been good and lovely. Blessed is the dying person who can cry. He is now in a most difficult phase. He is struggling to accept the fact that he is dying. Nobody can do this for him, but lovingly we ought to accompany him on that difficult journey as far as possible.

Albert Mauder thinks that this is the time when we can start talking with the dying person about God, and perhaps also pray together. It seems to me this would be right only with people who until then had no relationship with God. Persons who have been believing Christians, who have led a life of prayer and service, will want to claim the support and encouragement of the Lord much earlier, certainly at the time of learning of their fatal illness. In spite of their physical pain and the very real sorrow caused by saying good-bye to loved ones, they will appreciate it if you pray for them and with them.

On the other hand, a person who has prayed seldom or never, who lived more or less without God, may gradually become open to talking about God as he gives up the fight against death.

Even unbelievers are never quite able to shake off the

hunch that death is not the end and that, at least at the time of their departure, they ought to think about meeting God. It is possible that persons like that may suddenly express a surprising amount of interest to know more about God. They may want to discuss how they stand before him—whether what they have done is enough for their salvation. And if they don't say those actual words, their searching and burning eyes reveal their anxiety.

Blessed are we if in such situations we don't merely quote a few proof texts but actually pass on the wonderful comfort of the gospel which is for all lost sinners.

It is one of life's biggest miracles that many a confused and utterly lost person is able to find peace with God during the last hours of his life, and then proceed to walk confidently through the valley of death. Blessed are we if we can assume a constant attitude of unobtrusive but prayerful readiness to lead the dying person into that peace.

Once a person has accepted this divine comfort, he becomes quiet and submissive. As much as his strength permits, and if he can still speak, he will now give last instructions to those people taking care of him. If he expresses wishes about his funeral or other things that need to be taken care of after his passing, these should be written down so that he can actually see it. Insistent and awkward visitors should be kept away from him. New problems should not be discussed in the presence of the dying person. He has made his peace with God and man. Those who are with him feel that here is a person who in spite of much weakness is secure in the hands of God which extend far beyond death.

CHAPTER FOURTEEN

THE PROCESS OF DYING

There's an old song that says, "God spareth from a fast and sudden death." However, if we are always ready to die it would almost appear to be desirable to die quickly and painlessly—to be healthy one moment and dead the next. Wouldn't that be a lot better than slowly and painfully dying over a period of weeks or months? Of course, none of us can choose the way we are going to die. Actually there is something grand and powerful about consciously experiencing the dying process.

In case of a sudden death the relatives are hardly able to give any kind of assistance. On the other hand, in case of a slow death the relatives and friends participate in a meaningful way in the experience. If they are Christians, they are able to be of decisive assistance to the dying one.

We have talked about how the dying person experiences the various phases of dying up to the final acceptance of the fact of death. Now let us look at the process of dying itself.

Depending on the nature of the illness, the resistance of death, and the will to live, the actual dying can be a matter of minutes, hours, or even days. The first segment of dying frequently begins with the almost total disappearance of pain. The patient feels better but also weaker. There is little or no physical movement, and few if any words are spoken. Often the patient is thirsty. It is good always to have cold water within reach. Perhaps only the eyes speak anymore. For long periods of time the dying person may look into the faces of loved ones as if he wants to take their picture along. From the facial expressions of the dying one you will know whether he is afraid or feels secure. Accordingly, you can speak words of comfort, gratitude, or love. Don't speak loudly, but move close enough so that he understands every word.

Next comes a stage about which the surrounding people know very little, but which the dying one usually experiences very consciously. He doesn't seem to know where he is or what time of day it is. Space and time appear to be unimportant. Soon he will be in a world where all clocks have stopped, where time is no more. The room seems to float in empty space, and the immediate surroundings seem unclear and blurred. It seems as if God and eternity are reaching into this nether world of death.

This is the mysterious occurrence during which dying persons sometimes appear to relatives many miles away as if to bid them a last and final farewell. I don't believe we are dealing with merely spiritualistic phenomena nor merely with delusions of mentally deranged persons. There are too many reliable reports from sober and serious Christians for that. We have, perhaps, all heard of instances where soldiers who died in battle at the hour of their death visited their mother. Personally I find all the explanations given for this sort of puzzling phenomenon somehow less than satisfactory. I suspect that in death the spirit experiences mysterious steps of disengagement, and that eternity, which knows neither space nor time, for a brief moment bridges the threshold between our world and the next. However it may be, I believe it is wrong to want to investigate or intentionally initiate such experiences and phenomena.

In the third phase of dying the sense of sight disappears. The eyes remain closed, or when open cannot see anymore. This does not mean, however, that the dying person is sinking into pitch darkness. Persons who have gone through this phase and returned again to life have reported that they saw a strong light, while all around them everything else was dark. They felt an urge to stare into that light, or even move toward it. This could be the going through the valley of the shadow of death (Psalm 23:4). It is important that those who are with the dying person at this stage should read or quote portions of Scripture which speak about the God of light and about Jesus, the light of the world. The dying one is now like Peter who attempted to walk across the water to Jesus. As long as he looked at Jesus he was upheld and did not sink, but as soon as he looked at the rough water, he began to sink and fear gripped him. It is possible that those who do not know Jesus already see the grimaces of demons who are waiting to snatch them away.

Before and after this period of struggling with death it is possible that there will come a time of stressful death railing, a sort of rattling of the throat, of which the dying one is not aware. This marks the phase which those around the dying person usually consider as the end. The moment comes when breathing becomes weaker and stops entirely. The heart stops, like the pendulum of a clock that quits swinging. You will want to remain absolutely silent now. The most serious and holy moment has come: a person is leaving this world. It is as if a breath from another world were blowing through the room.

At this time the dying person experiences something like falling into eternity. He is not afraid, because there is also a feeling of liberation, of being carried upward. Many experience these moments with a clear consciousness although they seem to be unconscious. "This is it! Here I go!" There is no more anxiety, no fear. The struggle is over; all troubles are at an end.

We should know, however, that the final phase extends beyond the last breath which has been taken. The experts believe that consciousness does not disappear until two to five minutes after all vital signs have failed. It is quite possible, and in fact has been confirmed by those who were at the edge of death and returned again to life, that the dying person hears everything that is going on in the room around him although he may already seem dead. The ear seems still to be open. Persons who in a mysterious way returned to life reported later that they heard everything that was going on: the crying of the loved ones, the squabble of the heirs over a piece of jewelry, or the hospital that started its typical hectic business of disposing of the body.

That is why it is best to fill the moments immediately after the last breath has been taken with quoting Scripture or prayer. To start singing songs of praise and triumph can bring a breath of heaven into the room of this departing one. He takes these melodies with him, as it were, into his new world—a world of new reality, of real life without pain and death.

If one observes carefully the facial expressions of the dying person one realizes that in the moments following the taking of the last breath, something surely must be going on in the inner recesses of his soul. Painful and tense expressions fade away, the hands become limp. In part this is simply the death of the body which stops functioning. But there is more to it. It is as if the peace of God spreads over the face, and the person is released from any further pain and suffering.

"Blessed are the dead who die in the Lord."

CHAPTER FIFTEEN

CHRISTIAN ASSISTANCE TO THE DYING

Our world is a vast cemetery. Every day thousands of people die. Countless numbers of them die a terrible death, unhappy, without peace, lonely, and without comfort. Unfortunately, death in our modern hospitals is often shockingly miserable and without consolation.

Does it have to be like that? Do we Christians, who know Jesus as the conqueror of death, not have the privilege to help the dying, whether Christian or non-Christian, to face their last hour more confidently and hopefully? Certainly we must think more seriously and deeply about dying. And we should learn how to assist each other in the process of dying.

In my discussion of the different phases of dying I have already touched on this question of how we can best assist dying persons. Now I would like to give a few additional suggestions.

First of all, consider the patient's room. Most people would like to die at home, surrounded by their loved ones. I know that today, when so many people live in small apartments, that is difficult. But we should not be too quick to dismiss the idea. Perhaps it is possible after all if some changes are made, such as having a member of the family temporarily move out. Now and then even hospitals and doctors favor the idea of letting the patient go home to die. The room in which the patient will die, whether it is in the hospital or at home, should in any case be warm and cheerful. Fresh flowers that do not have too strong a fragrance help to add a touch of beauty. And a picture on the wall, if possible one of the dying person's favorites, should be hung where he can see it.

Try to create in the room of the dying person not a somber and sad environment but a festive atmosphere. Someone once commented that the room of a dying person should look like the room of a birthday child, spotlessly clean, decorated, and full of expectation.

In the room of the dying person we should avoid moving about silently for any prolonged period of time. It is also essential to avoid all animated conversation or whispering. We should act naturally toward the patient, and take time to talk with him. More and more we can try to steer the conversation to Jesus Christ, our Savior. In an unobtrusive way remind him of all of God's wonderful leadings in his life, helping establish a mood of thankfulness. If it seems that he is depressed or burdened by something, we ought to have a spiritual talk with him. If the dying person would like to make a last confession and asks for communion, we should arrange for this, making sure that nobody else is in the room and that there are no interruptions. In the case of communion, it is encouraging to have the loved ones participate.

If the dying extends over a period of days, we should attempt to communicate words of comfort to the patient every day. It is well to choose words of Scripture that are familiar and to read them from his favorite translation.

Such readings should be quite brief, but it is not too often to read three or four times a day.

If the agony of dying and inner restlessness increase, it will be necessary to have someone in the room around the clock. Ways have to be found for a familiar person to be with the dying person day and night. The illumination of the room should be according to the wishes of the patient. Maybe he will not want strong sunlight, and yet would like to keep the view to the outside open. Perhaps he would like to have a candle. A simple cross could be hung on the wall for the patient, which he can see without having to turn his head. As much as possible we should now stay right beside the bed, lightly holding the patient's hand, singing or reading a few verses of song which can very well be songs of joy and gratitude. Based on my own experience, I can also say that there is comfort in simply placing your hand now and then on the patient's forehead and saying, "The Lord bless you and keep you."

Often it is surprising how the patient, who so recently was still interested in life, the family, or the affairs of business, suddenly turns his back on all this and focuses only on preparations for entering into glory. With an almost incredible certainty he may say: "Let me go. I want to see Jesus. Do not stop me. The Lord is waiting for me!"

When that happens, there's only one thing to do. However much it may hurt, release the dying one and let him go home to his Lord and Maker. As Christians we have wonderful comfort. We can remember the words of the apostle Paul, "You will not be sad, as are those who have no hope. We believe that Jesus died and rose again, and so we believe that God will take back with Jesus those who have died believing in him" (1 Thessalonians 4:13-14, TEV).

CHAPTER SIXTEEN

THE SACREDNESS OF LIFE

God is your Creator and Sustainer of all life. That is why every human birth is a sacred event before which we should stand in awe. Some mothers reject the use of narcotics or anesthesia during the birth of a child. They know that giving birth is painful, but they want to experience this sacred event in full consciousness.

Dying is like that. After all, a person doesn't die as a victim of an accident or because of sickness, but because it is the will of God. In Psalm 90:3 we read: "Thou turnest man back to the dust, and sayest, 'Turn back, O children of men!' " That is a powerful word from the mouth of Moses. God alone has the right to let people die. He determines when the time for recall has come.

In Psalm 139:16 we read further, "Thy eyes beheld my unformed substance; in thy book were written, every one of them, the days that were formed for me, when as yet there was none of them." Are these not wonderful truths? Before my first day came God already had in his hand my calendar and all the events that were to follow. God knew the day of my birth and how long I would live. My time is in his hands. That is good, and that is how it should remain. God alone is to determine the length of my life. All the days of my life are written in his book.

These days, however, proud people that we are, we think we can determine everything ourselves. It appears that at last we have the possibility to snatch the control out of his hand. For example, we decide if and when we are going to have children. Now it is even possible to determine the sex of the child.

In time all this manipulation makes us feel a bit uneasy. Should we really use all the possibilities that are available to us? Sometimes one feels like crying out, "Hands off sacred things!" There are realms which must remain closed to our probing. We dare not do everything which theoretically we can do. From the Scriptures I conclude that human life is sacred. We dare not touch it. Only God has the right to determine the length of life. This is an area in which we are not consulted. How much clearer could it be said than it is said in Exodus 20:13— "You shall not kill"?

In the Corinthian church some people insisted that only the spirit of a person is important. The body can be destroyed without the actual person suffering any consequences, they said. Paul wrote to these people: "Do you not know that you are God's temple and that God's Spirit dwells in you? If any one destroys God's temple, God will destroy him. For God's temple is holy, and that temple you are" (1 Corinthians 3:16-17).

In other words, the body belongs to the Lord. We cannot do with it as we please. That is why I think that as Christians we have to say no to every form of murder and killing of persons. We cannot agree with modern theories which say that there are no absolutes, that everything is relative, and one has to act according to a given situation.

Some go so far as to say that under certain circumstances, if the motive is love, killing a person is a good thing.

There is the example of a mother who smothers her own child because its crying would have attracted the persecutors to a group of fleeing refugees. The murder of her own child is celebrated as a heroic deed. But isn't that terrible? That is no way to solve problems. There is something much worse than being killed—being a killer! You know the story of Cain and Abel, the story of the one who was killed and the one who did the killing. Which of the two was in greater danger? It is obvious that God regarded Cain, the killer, as the one in greatest danger. God seemed more concerned about Cain than about Abel. With God, killing is a lot worse than being killed.

I'm convinced that there are a number of things which we should not do under any circumstances. There are divine, immutable laws. These eternal laws cannot be set aside, not even by the highest command—the command of love. In fact, in and through love they are to be fulfilled. Job once said he had taken a vow with his eyes. Under no circumstances did he want to see certain pictures. Perhaps we should take a holy vow with our heart—a vow that certain deeds we will not contemplate, let alone carry out.

It seems to me that as Christians we need to say a loud and clear "No" to abortion and an equally loud and clear "No" to euthanasia, the so-called mercy killing. We dare not shorten human life. God alone has the right to cut the thread of life. Our task is to maintain life.

Normally all people have the justifiable wish for a long and fulfilled life. Believers in Old Testament times considered it a special favor from God if they were given a long life. A long and well-rounded life is a justified wish.

The psalmist expresses that in the request: "O my God . . . take me not hence in the midst of my days" (Psalm 102:24).

To live long and be happy is beautiful—but it is not the highest and the best that there is. It isn't even a worthy goal of life. Paul actually wrote once, "To die would be gain for me." One can wish for a long life. One ought to take care of oneself and maintain life, but not at any price. Life is not the highest good. Nor is health more important than anything else, even though many people say so. Health is a treasure, but it dare not be bought at any price. It is interesting that King Solomon did not ask God for a long life, but for a wise heart.

We should remember these basic principles and divine laws also when we consider one of the growing problems of our time: the new form of fear of death which many people nowadays are suffering under. They are not afraid to lose their life. They are not afraid of the judgment of God which awaits them after death. They are afraid of a long and senseless process of dying. They ask themselves, "When my hour has come, will they let me die in peace? Or will they keep my body alive with sophisticated inventions even if I yearn to go home?" Relatives at the bedside of their loved ones ask, "Is it necessary to have this cruel and painful extension of life? Why not leave well enough alone?" And the doctor replies: "No, under no circumstances. I have taken an oath to preserve and save human life with all my power."

Does a person have the right to die his own death? Can he request that people stop artificially prolonging his life? Can an incurable person perhaps even make an end to his own life? We will talk about these questions in the next chapter.

CHAPTER SEVENTEEN

THE RIGHT TO DIE

The psalmist wrote, "My times are in thy hand" (Psalm 31:15). I believe it is good to keep that in mind. "Lord, my time shall remain in your hands. You determine the length of my life."

But let us be careful not to condemn people who have decided otherwise. For example, there is an incurable sick person who faces a horrible life. Because of the fear of pain and also out of sympathy for his loved ones who will have to continue bearing the load of taking care of him, he consciously shortens his life. There are also innumerable people who in desperation choose death in order to escape a disastrous future. We know that these people are in the merciful hands of God. We have no right to throw stones. These people have already suffered enough. Nevertheless, the basic question has to be asked, "Is it right to terminate one's own life in suicide?"

Elsewhere in this book I have tried to show that there is such a thing as a "blessed death," a dying in the Lord. I do not merely mean that death is the gateway to heavenly bliss, but that the process of dying itself can be a blessed and hallowed experience. A consciously experienced dy-

ing, a victory over the fear of death, and a peaceful farewell from this world can be a crowning completion of life.
In fact, it can be the pinnacle. Dying like that, at the conclusion of a fruitful life, can be compared to a grand finale
at the end of a symphony—everything would be incomplete if the closing piece were missing. There is such a
thing as final clarity and illumination, deep peace of God,
and knowing something about the mysteries of life that is
granted only in the last moments of conscious experience
between life and death.

There is also something lofty about dying. One should
wish for oneself and others a truly hallowed dying. In
reverence, one ought to stand at attention before it. In old
prayers we find many times the sentence, "Lord, give me
a life pleasing to you, and give me also a perfect death."
Hidden in that prayer is the wish that through the
experience of death one might become fully mature and
finally ready for eternity. Under certain circumstances, if
one does not allow a person to complete his life in peace
and harmony, one robs him of something very vital. In
dying lies the possibility of achieving something which
was not possible to achieve during a lifetime. Perhaps it is
necessary to make something right. When a person faces
the dark gate of death and beyond that begins to see the
light of glory and eternity, he may be startled and ask,
"What is my real condition? Is it good enough for salvation; and if I'm going to be saved, for what reason? Why?
Because I was so good?"

When finally there is nothing left as basis for salvation
other than the name of Jesus, one stands there poor and
naked—and indescribably happy! Then the dying of a
child of God can become for the loved ones an
unforgettable experience. It is possible that the day of

death may be of such wonderful splendor that at least for the time being there is little thought about the pain of parting.

Many people have testified that the dying of a member of their family has changed their whole life. When a child of God gets ready to depart this world the angels are present. The Spirit of peace fills every heart.

That is why it is regrettable when one denies a person the opportunities of passing through the fiery ordeal of the normal process of dying. He has been robbed of a raw, but yet precious, experience.

We said earlier that everyone has the right to live. That is clear. The laws of our country protect the right to live. The police intervene if a life is threatened. But these days one almost needs to demand a new right—the right to be allowed to die. This right is nowhere protected by the police. The patient actually has to fight to be allowed to die his own death.

I read about an old baker who regularly had to have injections in order to continue living. One day he looked the doctor in the eye and said with great calmness, "Doctor, please leave me alone. Stop this tampering." And the doctor said, "Okay, if that's what you wish." He took his syringe and needle, and left. After a few days the old baker died quietly. They found his much-used book of prayer on his bedcovers.

Don't you agree that is how one ought to be allowed to die? With a clear and conscious decision: I'm ready, please, now let me go?

Every person should have the right to die like that. What prevents one from doing it? In the first place, there is all that deceit and lying of the relatives and those who take care of the patient. Quite consciously they feed the dying person a string of lies. Even on the day of his death they say, "Tomorrow will surely be a better day for you." Sometimes people even boast at the funeral: "He didn't even know that he was going to die."

This kind of deception spoils everything that God was going to give through the painful experience of dying.

In the second place, some doctors make a peaceful dying experience difficult. They treat the patient as if he were some kind of machine that needed to be fixed. One is almost powerless against the materialism of the doctors. Nevertheless, as Christians we need to ask ourselves what we can do to correct these conditions. I think that to safeguard the right to normal dying we must observe the following basic principles:

1. The patient has to know the truth. If he doesn't know that he is going to die, he misses a chance to consciously process his dying. It just isn't right to cheat him out of the benefit of experiencing a blessed dying.

2. Only the patient may decide. Only the patient has the right to determine whether and when to continue all those life-supporting efforts. Neither the doctors nor the family has the right to conclude, "Now we let him die. Let's pull the plug."

3. And it should be clear, of course, that we dare not speed up the process of dying. Speeding up the dying would mean, for example, that we give the patient an injection that would kill him. This is in stark contradiction to God's command.

Briefly, a few comments about difficult borderline cases. What is to be done if it is proven that there is extensive brain damage? With the help of life-supporting techniques the body functions, such as heart and lungs, can continue to function for years, but for all practical purposes the person is a vegetable.

Or what about a senile person in the old people's home? He doesn't know his own family anymore and takes absolutely no part in life. He lies there day in and day out like a clump of half dead matter. Shall we let him die? Shall we perhaps even give a bit of assistance so that he dies sooner? What about completely paralyzed and totally disabled children who vegetate like animals? Should we not say, let these poor people die?

I would like to give a warning. Please don't interfere too soon! And in any case, never because of your own convenience. If someone in the family needs our care and attention throughout life it means we will have to take ourselves in hand and ask God again and again to give us the grace and courage to say, "Yes." Beautiful dreams and wishes are destroyed. Consciously we accept the responsibility of caring for the patient over many years. But lo and behold, these years become a bit of heaven. Sometimes the necessary efforts may lead to exhaustion and bring us to the edge of a nervous breakdown. But I know parents who testify, "Our incurable child is our biggest treasure; he is a gift from God." And this sick child also has a right to live and to die on his own. This too is in the will and plan of God.

CHAPTER EIGHTEEN

EXPECTING TO DIE

Lord, let me know my end, and what is the measure of my days; let me know how fleeting my life is!" (Psalm 39:4).

Your life is short. It races along. You are a temporary guest on earth. Think about that. James warns the busy and preoccupied people saying, "You make big plans extending over a long period of time, and yet you do not even know whether you will still be alive tomorrow."

At a recent meeting we made plans for the program the following year. I felt a bit uneasy about that. I had to ask myself whether we would actually live to see the realization of the things we were planning. Jesus warns us not to be tardy in clearing up an unsettled dispute: "Make friends quickly with your accuser, while you are going with him" (Matthew 5:25). Again and again the Word of God calls us not to forget the fact that we must die, and include it in all our planning.

To think about dying certainly doesn't mean to be sad all the time, but rather to live in light of that reality, to live right. Sometimes when I admire the abundance of spring blossoms I ask myself whether this is perhaps the last time that I will see them. We really should enjoy all the beauty of the earth much more consciously. We should accept it as a gift from God and be thankful. Just because life is fleeting and brief is no reason to be filled with panic. While we enjoy all the lovely things in the world, we should also practice letting go of them. We close doors that we will never open again. We leave places that we will never visit again. We say good-bye to our friends for good. That needs to be practiced. It is so easy to drag all kinds of unfinished business around with us. It becomes impossible to give ourselves fully to the future because we are not able to let go of the past.

Some of us may have to consult a psychiatrist and ask him to help us to untangle and untie the old knots. But sincere Christians know that with God forgiveness and complete cleansing is possible. Old and messy affairs can be blotted out. Then it isn't necessary to worry or be anxious anymore. Jesus has cleared up everything that we couldn't handle ourselves. Now it is done and we can go on with a light step and a clear conscience.

Sometimes we cannot completely resolve a quarrel or a fight because we cannot force other people to change themselves. Paul became reconciled to the fact that he had to deal with false brothers who hindered his work behind his back. He couldn't change that. As long as he lived and worked he had to be firm and resist them. To think about dying in such a case means to persevere for yet a short time, "hang in there" until the Lord himself changes things.

To think about dying means that first things come first. For truly vibrant Christians this means, of course, glorifying the name of Jesus Christ through obedience to his Great Commission. It is wonderful to meet old people whose hearts burn for mission. There seems to be a holy impatience about them. They have so little time left and there is so much to do.

To think about dying also means helping others and accepting the help of others. It is difficult for strong and proud people to accept the help of others when they are no longer able to take care of themselves. First of all, we should think about the fact that lonely, weak, and dying persons need our assistance—and soon it will be our turn to accept assistance from others.

To think about dying could also mean that we do something about the many people who die lonely and alone. Thousands die without any kind of assistance. No one hears their groans; no one relieves their fears. Sometimes they are not even discovered by neighbors until a few days after their death. We should be more concerned about lonely people, and we should also prepare for our own dying so that it won't be in utter loneliness.

To think about dying also means that we think about the possibility of a sudden death. The possibility of being swept away by instant death has greatly increased in our time. Every ride in the car could be our last one. Crime and natural catastrophes have increased. And then there is the possibility of suddenly being struck down by a heart attack.

How gladly we would like to dispel such thoughts. We think it won't hit us. And suddenly death strikes down one of our friends or acquaintances and we have to admit, it could have been me. It can be a salutary experience for us to escape death by a hair's breadth. It reminds us that we always live on the edge of the grave, that we ought to live with the expectation of dying, and that every new day is an extension of God's grace. We should often sing:

I owe the Lord a morning song
Of gratitude and praise,
For the kind mercy he has shown
In length'ning out my days.

Finally, to think about dying means not to gather up treasures on earth. Jesus expressly forbade that (Matthew 6:19). Our charity and concern for the poor should provide treasures for us in heaven. How did he mean that? Presumably that we should not only give out of our abundance, but dip into our capital reserves. We should not only do good with that which we can easily spare. We are to share our bread with the hungry. We are to give to the poor to the extent that we will need to reduce our own consumption. The first Christians did that and none of them ever suffered need.

Again and again Jesus warns us to seek first the kingdom of God, to do that which has eternal worth. Attempt to live a lifestyle pleasing to God. It is possible to do mighty deeds which heaven won't even record. These "mighty deeds" aren't necessarily bad, but on the other hand, they don't do much ultimate good either. On the other hand, deeds done in love and in faith (rescue services of all kinds, for example), are pleasing to God. Not even a cup of cold water will go unnoticed, which doesn't mean, of course, that we should always and almost compulsively be out there "doing good." Only that which is done out of compassion for others and out of gratitude to God is of lasting value.

If we think about God we cannot become lazy and inactive even when old age appears. In the marketplace of the world they don't want old people anymore. And we are happy with those people who have worked faithfully and hard up to the age of 65 or so, and are at last relieved of their daily task. But after that, most of them are still in a position to do something else, some good deed. Unfortunately, most people by that time have become so inflexible that they cannot find suitable placement.

Now if they would be prepared to move, say at the age of 60 to a different location or even overseas, they could still be a real blessing to many people in the evening of their life. I know personally several people who after 65 tried something entirely new and different, and who testified that their last years were even better and richer than the years of their prime. And if at last you really can't do anything anymore, then concentrate more consciously than ever on the big journey ahead of you. To think about dying then means to remain faithful to the Lord until death. "He who endures to the end will be saved" (Matthew 10:22).

CHAPTER NINETEEN

ORIENTATION FOR HEAVEN

To think about dying does not only mean thinking about the big journey ahead of us, nor only thinking about all that which yet awaits us before we are called home. Those who think about dying should also think about that which follows. The closer we get to heaven the more we should orientate ourselves to it. When we plan to take a major trip we get a map and a prospectus and study it carefully. Several years ago my wife and I visited South America. We carried with us quite a thick traveler's guidebook and every time before we boarded another plane we studied carefully what was said about the new country we were going to. Where will we land? What is important to see? How do people live there? How do we need to behave in order not to give offense?

But why are we so reluctant to gather information about heaven? If we really believe that someday we are going to land there, why do we know so little about what to expect there? I know, it isn't quite that simple. My wife and I had a few big surprises in South America in spite of our careful preparations.

Heaven is not only a strange continent but another

world. The biblical descriptions about heaven are difficult to interpret. It is necessary to persevere in learning to understand biblical language. I confess that I am very much interested in heaven. I consider it my true homeland, my future place of residence. I would like to know more about my new domicile. What about the streets of gold and the pearly gates of the new Jerusalem? What about the tree of life and the water of life? But what is more important? How will heaven be populated? Whom can I expect to meet there? Will I be completely among strangers? How can I feel at home then?

Of course we all expect to see Jesus face to face in heaven. But do we really know him? Are we familiar with his language and his nature even if we have never seen his face? Will we be able to go joyfully right up to him? Of course we have our notions about him. We have a hunch what he must be like because we have heard about him. We have sung songs about him. We even pray to him—and yet we know him so little.

And how well do we know the angels about whom the Bible speaks so much? Is the matter settled if we smile and lay all those angel stories aside as legends, as remnants of antiquated thinking? The Bible seems to indicate that at death we are going to be taken away by angels. Why don't we at least get all the pieces of information together about the angels that the Bible has to offer?

I know that a lot of nonsense has been said and written about heaven and things beyond the grave. That has spoiled it for many of us to dig in and try to find out what information really is available. If the experts can't even agree, why should we bother? So we tend to forget about things that far in the future and concentrate on what is at hand.

But what is the consequence of that? Because we talk so little about heaven, the false teachers and godless people exaggerate and have a heyday. At the moment it is fashionable to write about the spirit world. Even the secular illustrated magazines do not hesitate to write about this topic. We Christians had hardly spoken on the subject because we wanted to be modern. The consequence has been that twisted and mixed-up people took these topics out of our hands and have done a great deal of mischief with them. Because we have been accused of talking too much about the other world we have almost eliminated the word "heaven" from our vocabulary. If only our opponents would be right when they accuse us of talking too much about the next world, about heaven. But unfortunately, it isn't true.

And finally this. Christians can't very well think about dying without at least considering the possibility that they may have to die for the sake of Christ. Paul wrote, "I die every day!" (1 Corinthians 15:31). Because he served the Lord he faced death daily. Every day he was totally committed to Jesus Christ, living and serving him, and always expecting that this could mean his end.

Jesus predicted that the struggle would be hard and that for his sake we might be asked to lay down our life. We will meet the same hatred as our Master met. What they have done to him, they will also do to us. In Romans 8:36 we are told that we will not only die for Jesus once, but "for thy sake we are being killed all the day long." This being killed all the day long is a continuous process on the road of our discipleship. And what does the world think when they kill us? The Bible says, "We are regarded as sheep for the slaughter." Being killed is, however, quite normal for a sheep that is raised to be slaughtered. It is of no use to cry out or protest. If somewhere there is a flock of sheep, it is a foregone conclusion that sooner or later the turn to be slaughtered comes to every sheep. It's just a question of which sheep goes today and which one goes tomorrow. Nobody makes a fuss about that.

That is also how it is with the Christian. Sometimes death strikes a few and at other times it strikes hundreds and even thousands at once—"Regarded as sheep for the slaughter." Jesus also said that those who kill Christians will not have a bad conscience. In fact, they expect that God will reward them for it.

I have observed a number of incidents lately which indicate that the hatred for the Christian is increasing. Even in our so-called free countries people are upset and angry at Christians. If a spiritual Christian dares to speak out against the crass immorality rampant nowadays, he is immediately shouted down. Many brothers and sisters experience a wall of rejection at their places of work, or even at home, and sometimes the hatred breaks through: "Away with these Christians. Away with these impossible critics."

The autonomous man of today will not tolerate the idea of being subject to the higher authority of God.

Peter wrote almost 2,000 years ago to a young Christian congregation: "Beloved, do not be surprised at the fiery ordeal which comes upon you to prove you, as though something strange were happening to you" (1 Peter 4:12).

There are signs that indicate that time is running out. Before the end comes, however, it is likely that the blood of Christians will also flow in our Western world.

To think about dying, therefore, includes for us accepting the idea that possibly we too may have to suffer and die for the sake of Christ. If we are not ready for that, we will certainly fail and betray our Lord. We will keep silent when we should speak. If that has happened already we should repent and pledge our allegiance to Christ, a faithfulness unto death.

A moment ago we said "For thy sake we are being killed all the day long; we are regarded as sheep to be slaughtered." Do you know what is written before and after that passage in the Bible? Ponder it carefully:

> Who shall separate us from the love of Christ? Shall tribulation, or distress, or persecution, or famine, or nakedness, or peril, or sword? As it is written, "For thy sake we are being killed all the day long; we are regarded as sheep to be slaughtered." No, in all these things we are more than conquerors through him who loved us. For I am sure that neither death, nor life, nor angels, nor principalities, nor things present, nor things to come, nor powers, nor height, nor depth, nor anything else in all creation, will be able to separate us from the love of God in Christ Jesus our Lord. Romans 8:35-39.

Other Herald Press Resources on Death

Danger in the Pines by Ruth Nulton Moore. Juvenile novel of 14-year-old Jeff Dawson coming to terms with his mother's new friend after his father's tragic death. 160 pages.

Empty Arms by Mary Joyce Rae. Visitation Pamphlet for those who lose their child at birth or through miscarriage. 16 pages.

Facing Terminal Illness by Mark Peachey. A pastor's candid thoughts as he struggles with terminal cancer. 72 pages.

Grief's Slow Work by Harold Bauman. Visitation Pamphlet explaining the process one normally goes through following bereavement. 16 pages.

Helping Children Cope with Death by Robert V. Dodd. Observations by an experienced pastor. 56 pages.

In Grief's Lone Hour by John M. Drescher. Visitation Pamphlet providing understanding of the grief experience. 16 pages.

Ken's Hideout by Dorothy Hamilton. Juvenile novel of the anxieties of a boy who lost a parent and faces the possibility of a stepparent. 88 pages.

Like a Shock of Wheat by Marvin Hein. Christian meditations on death. 192 pages.

My Comforters by Helen Good Brenneman. Meditations for those whose life has been changed by death, disease, or disaster. 80 pages.

My Walk Through Grief by Janette Klopfenstein. The story of a young mother's sudden loss of her husband. 120 pages.

Morning Joy by Helen Good Brenneman. Meditations for those who have suffered loss—whether it be death, divorce, health, or economic disaster. 80 pages.

Tell Me About Death, Mommy, by Janette Klopfenstein. A young widow's story of helping her sons cope with their father's death. 112 pages.